CHOSEN MEMORIES

CHOSEN MEMORIES
Contemporary Latin American Art from the Patricia Phelps de Cisneros Gift and Beyond

INÉS KATZENSTEIN

THE MUSEUM OF MODERN ART, NEW YORK

Chosen Memories: Contemporary Latin American Art from the Patricia Phelps de Cisneros Gift and Beyond presents recent art that looks, perhaps unexpectedly, back in time. But as the Brazilian photographer Rosângela Rennó recently said, "History is a living organism, perpetually reread and reassessed." In a moment like ours, of compounding crises and collective questioning, the works in this exhibition offer crucial ways to both reread and reassess the past and to imagine new futures.

This timely exhibition celebrates the gift of ninety works of contemporary art from Latin America given to the Museum by Trustee Patricia Phelps de Cisneros in 2018. It follows MoMA's 2019 exhibition *Sur moderno: Journeys of Abstraction*, an expansive presentation that commemorated Patty's earlier gift of geometric abstraction from mid-century Latin America. Together, these two gifts demonstrate not only Patty's generosity and long-term commitment to the Museum, but also the lucidity of her vision. Over the course of five decades, she assembled a collection of Latin American art that has, it is no exaggeration to say, fundamentally helped to change our understanding of the art of the region—and not just in this country but around the world, including Latin America. With its favoring of the rational and the conceptual over the exotic and the fantastical, the Colección Cisneros has remained remarkably coherent, especially given the broad range of geographies, artistic practices, and eras represented; and it is this heterogeneity within a cohesive whole that allows for so many possible conversations across time. Just as the works selected for this exhibition stand in dialogue with the art and cultural histories that came before them, so too does Patty's Contemporary Gift stand in a rich and textured dialogue with the Modern Gift that preceded it. *Sur moderno* asked the question of where the hopes placed in modernity's great transformations might lead; *Chosen Memories* proposes something of an answer, through works that think critically about those promises of progress and offer new ways of coping with a challenging present.

Encompassing the work of approximately forty artists from the past several decades, this exhibition takes as its starting point a core group of thirty-five paintings, photographs, videos, slide projections, and sculptures from the donation. It brings them together with works from the Museum's renowned collection of Latin American art, as well as a number of loans (including from Patty's daughter, Adriana Cisneros de Griffin), commissions, and recent acquisitions made possible by Patty's leadership of the Latin American and Caribbean Fund.

I would like to thank Inés Katzenstein, Curator of Latin American Art and Director of the Patricia Phelps de Cisneros Research Institute for the Study of Art from Latin America, and Julia Detchon, Curatorial Assistant in the Department of Drawings and Prints, for organizing a provocative show around one of the multiple through lines that emerge from the gift. Surely this is only the first of many such thematic presentations to come.

We thank our lenders and the artists who participated in this exhibition and publication, and we are profoundly grateful to The International Council of The Museum of Modern Art and donors to the Museum's Annual Exhibition Fund for their support.

Glenn D. Lowry
The David Rockefeller Director
The Museum of Modern Art, New York

Plate 1

Thiago Rocha Pitta (Brazilian, born 1980)
Herança (*Heritage*). 2007
16mm film transferred to video (color, sound),
11 min.

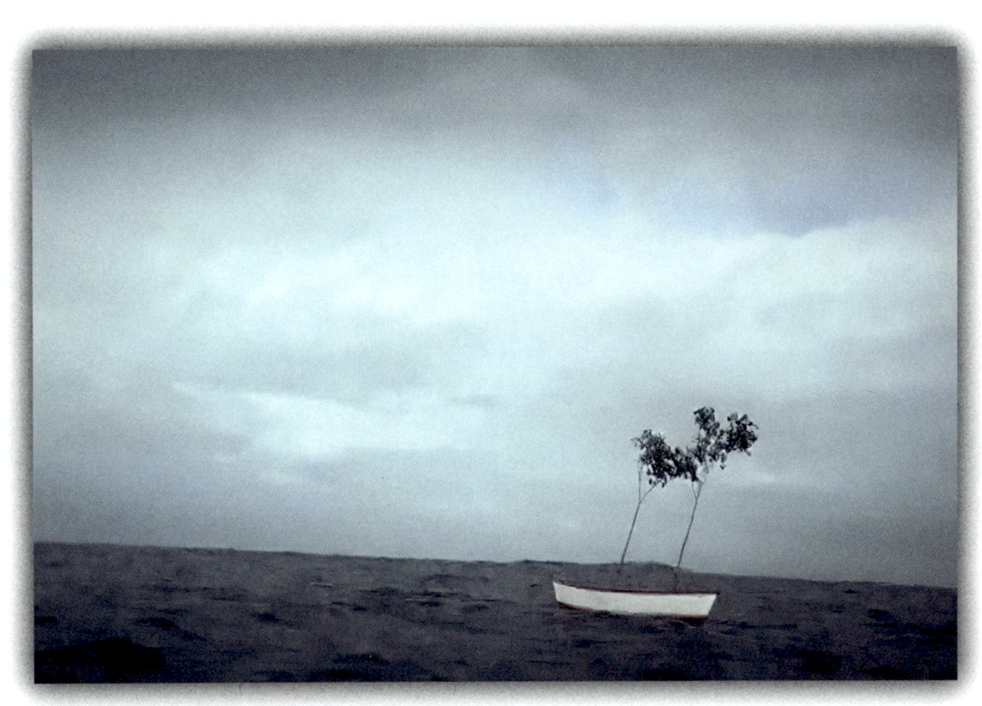

CHOSEN MEMORIES

Contemporary Latin American Art from the Patricia Phelps de Cisneros Gift and Beyond

INÉS KATZENSTEIN

Chosen Memories emerged from a close study of the Latin American artworks that came to The Museum of Modern Art in 2016 through a donation from the Colección Patricia Phelps de Cisneros. This examination led to an initial concept that eventually drew in other works from the Museum's collection as well as selected loans. The core pieces chosen through our research revolve around a theoretical axis that might be described as "out of joint," as it asserts contemporaneity through a commitment to history. Regardless of the date their works were created, the artists in this exhibition seek to affect the present (both theirs and ours) by drawing very specific connections to the past. Their efforts take different forms—recording resonances, revisiting controversies, honoring the dead, repeating events that have already occurred, working deliberately to affirm the continuity of specific cultural traditions—like a piece of embroidery that reaches backward, or a cavernous valley, where echoes bring to the present, in successive waves, cries and songs from the past.

The artists' drive to connect selectively with history converges with the present in an attempt to create a situation of "non-contemporaneity with itself of the living present," as Jacques Derrida put it.[1] Their quest, however, is neither nostalgic nor reactionary nor formalistic.[2] For all the artists in the exhibition—who span several generations—the interest in what has already happened is motivated by a critical and reconstructive spirit, a vital historicism. History emerges as an essential source for the construction of an ethical sense of belonging in the present but also as a path toward confronting the falsehoods of received histories and the weight of hegemonic concepts of progress.

Dating from the mid-1980s to the present, the works in the exhibition address many of the same issues raised by postmodernism, which challenged the linear narrative of modern art history. However, I think it is more revealing to contextualize the broad spectrum of artwork here by shedding light on more recent debates that have been slowly—but drastically—transforming the parameters not only of Latin American art but of the entire art world. These include key phenomena of our current moment, such as the changing perception of time brought on by the environmental crisis, the influence of decolonial theory and its radical critique of Western binarism, and the simultaneous cultural processes of homogenization and heterogeneity that globalization has wrought.

This exhibition invites us to consider the slow demise of the notion of history as a past time or an archive that we access and use from a "now" that is a relative future. I am referring not to the concept of the death of ideologies—what Francis Fukuyama called the "end of history"—but rather to the fact that history, for these artists, lives *with* and *in* the present, in a way that is powerful, enigmatic, and fundamentally transformative, and is expressed through rituals of repetition, exorcism, and myth-making.

Proposing dialogues between works created in Latin America in very different historical and national contexts over a period of more than thirty years, the exhibition starts with a mid-1990s piece by Rosângela Rennó shown in dialogue with one by Sofía Gallisá Muriente, addressing similar concerns, but more than twenty years later. Rennó is a Brazilian artist who, since the late 1980s, has explored the history of images by studying photographic archives that were regarded in their time as minor or unimportant and, as a result, were later neglected or discarded. Her *Wedding Landscape* (1996, plate 72) is a transparent acrylic structure containing strips of negatives salvaged from a portrait studio in Cuba. Capturing hundreds of wedding portraits, most of the photographs were shot following strict guidelines. Intrigued by the various forms photography may take, Rennó plays here with the

1 Jacques Derrida, *Specters of Marx: The State of Debt, the Work of Mourning and the New International* (New York: Routledge, 1994), 22.

2 The idea of the artist as historian became a topic of debate in the United States around 2015. Claire Bishop was the most emphatic critic of this kind of historicism. See, for example, Claire Bishop, "History Depletes Itself," *Artforum* 54, no. 1 (September 2015): 324.

possibility of creating a landscape with the almost topographic texture of the negatives. But, more importantly, she is fascinated by the status of photographic archives and their role in building collective memory. As the artist points out:

> Some [of my] works from the nineties were connected to the precarity of our archives here in Brazil and to a certain "historical amnesia" that was aggravated by our twenty-year-plus dictatorship [1964–85] and has recurred in the last few decades. The construction of history in our country relies heavily on weak evidence and imprecise documents, as well as entire archives deliberately destroyed or abandoned, because it doesn't seem to matter whether the story is told truthfully.[3]

Gallisá Muriente's *Asimilar y destruir* (*Assimilate and Destroy*) (2019, plate 67) comes out of her longstanding research into the relationship between politics and memory in Puerto Rico. The work is an enlarged projection of a 16mm film negative that the artist had buried in a vat filled with salt, in an effort to precipitate the kind of deterioration that archival materials undergo naturally in tropical climates. The children in the film, playing on an ice-skating rink, are almost completely shrouded by a layer of fractal-like forms produced by the salt, as if they were covered in bits of snow. The work tests chemical processes that literally corrode the possibility of keeping collective memory alive through archives.

These two works introduce the exhibition and its themes by embodying the fundamental tension between preservation and productive forgetting, as well as the suspension of linear time. The exhibition then unfolds into three main sections—Returns, Reverberations, and Kinships—which are also reflected in the following pages. The artists included in the first section look at the long histories of coloniality in the region by questioning received modes of representing nature; those in the second address various forms of engaging creatively and even disruptively with cultural heritage; and those in the third focus on the importance of building critical memories and feelings of belonging through "caretaking precious kin that come to us in diverse ways."[4]

3   Interview with Rosângela Rennó by Elise Y. Chagas and Madeline Murphy Turner, July 7, 2020, conducted for the Cisneros Institute project "Study of the Patricia Phelps de Cisneros Gift" (hereafter cited as "Study of the Cisneros Gift"). See "History Is a Living Organism: A Conversation with Rosângela Rennó," *MoMA Magazine*, September 6, 2002, https://www.moma.org/magazine/articles/769.

4   Kim TallBear, "Making Love and Relations beyond Settler Sex and Family," in *The Material Kinship Reader: Material Beyond Extraction and Kinship Beyond the Nuclear Family*, ed. Kris Dittel and Clementine Edwards (Rotterdam: Onomatopee, 2022), 237.

I

Returns

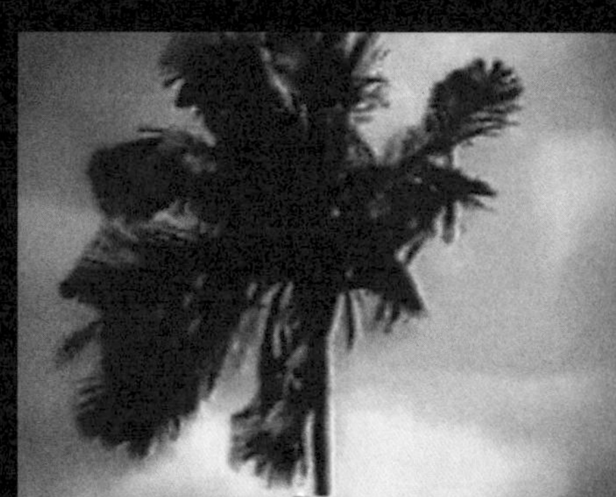

José Alejandro Restrepo. *Paso del Quindío I (Quindío Pass I)*. 1992

I

Resisting the hierarchical terms of cultural and political relations with Europe and the United States has been one of the most enduring projects of modernity in Latin America for many years. Celebrated early examples of this resistant perspective include Joaquín Torres-García's inverted map of South America, from 1943, and Oswald de Andrade's 1928 *Manifesto Antropófago* (*Anthropophagic Manifesto*), along with the cultural movement it spawned. In the 1990s this impulse gained new energy, and discussion of the modern-day repercussions of the colonization of the Americas became one of the central points of what, here, we understand as a radical redefinition of both art and politics.

The first section of the exhibition includes several artists who have focused on dismantling the effects that the colonial gaze has had (and still has) on the representation and perception of their territories and their history. Most of them have conducted research in historical archives (museums, libraries, collections of photographs or maps), places they see as the repositories of histories that continue to reverberate in the present. Embracing a variety of practices, they engage in performative or symbolic acts of repetition, self-sacrifice, or inversion of perspective, and work to reclaim forms of heritage that have long been excluded from the hegemonic narratives of art history. In all cases, their goal is to generate a critical friction that will help to repair dependencies, appropriations, and experiences of being silenced.

The Colombian artist José Alejandro Restrepo has consistently studied the intellectual construct of his country's landscape as well as the struggles, erasures, and negotiations resulting from the violent encounters between science, religion, and myth during colonization. A pioneer in Latin American video art, Restrepo combines historical research with an ever-evolving sculptural experimentation with monitors, projections, and other elements. His works synthesize a wide spectrum of primary sources—from old etchings to press clippings and television footage—to shed light on, and thus dismantle, hegemonic narratives about the history of Colombia and to recover forgotten histories.

In *Paso del Quindío I* (*Quindío Pass I*) (1992, plate 16), Restrepo embarks on an experience of return. The work reconstructs a journey undertaken in 1801 by Alexander von Humboldt, the celebrated German geographer, naturalist, and explorer, who from 1799 to 1805 documented a vast expanse of American lands including Cuba, Mexico, Venezuela, and the Andes from Peru north. Composed of seventeen monitors with black-and-white images placed at different levels of a pyramidal set of steps, Restrepo's video-sculpture shows his own 1991 footage of his ascent, by foot, of the titular Andes mountain pass, known for its technical climbing difficulty and its strategic importance in the challenging history of integrating the country's various geographical regions. Each step of the pyramid corresponds to a level of the mountain, from 2,600 to 11,500 feet (800 to 3,500 meters), up to the summit of the pass.

"*Paso del Quindío* is like the last in a set of Russian nesting dolls," Restrepo says. "Humboldt made a sketch in 1801; almost ten years later, he gave it to Joseph Anton Koch in Rome so he could make the final drawing; that drawing was then given to Christian Friedrich Traugott Duttenhofer in Stuttgart to make a print." He explains that "Humboldt's memory and compositional criteria were used throughout. He gave precise instructions: 'Put a fallen trunk with orchids here and there,' 'Put backlit plants in the foreground,' etc. The final print…is a palimpsest, a bricolage, a montage" (fig. 1).[5]

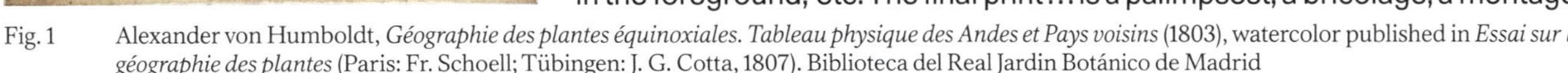
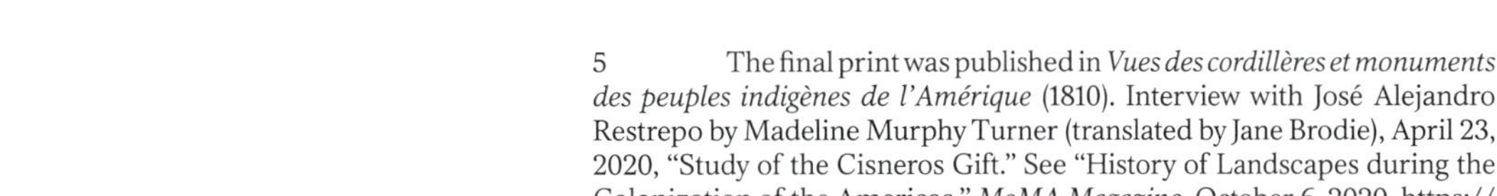

Fig. 1   Alexander von Humboldt, *Géographie des plantes équinoxiales. Tableau physique des Andes et Pays voisins* (1803), watercolor published in *Essai sur la géographie des plantes* (Paris: Fr. Schoell; Tübingen: J. G. Cotta, 1807). Biblioteca del Real Jardín Botánico de Madrid

Restrepo's piece presents the mountain-climbing journey as a way of joining multiple representations of Colombia's steep geography. The work, he tells us, is "one more interpretation in a long chain. In the end, no true original is left, just

5   The final print was published in *Vues des cordillères et monuments des peuples indigènes de l'Amérique* (1810). Interview with José Alejandro Restrepo by Madeline Murphy Turner (translated by Jane Brodie), April 23, 2020, "Study of the Cisneros Gift." See "History of Landscapes during the Colonization of the Americas," *MoMA Magazine*, October 6, 2020, https://www.moma.org/magazine/articles/431.

copies of copies, reworkings of reworkings, making images to read the world. The victor's images become the reference images, and his systems of representation become the models used to capture the world visually."[6] Confronting the notion of "discovery" that is part of the official history of the American landscape constructed by European explorers, Restrepo proposes his own ascent, one that is elusive, perhaps even distanced, one more in a long line of versions and distortions shaped by the nature of "copies of copies." By repeating the journey, he both parodies and challenges the foundational nature of colonial archives.[7]

Some years earlier, the Argentine artist Leandro Katz had already begun to highlight the role of European mediation in the construction of our image of the Americas. With the voyages he would undertake for The Catherwood Project (plates 2–8, 12–14), he conducted an extensive inquiry into history by traveling to the same destinations visited and documented by European explorers.[8] Like Restrepo, he complemented his documentary research with travel; but for Katz, it was also crucial to document himself in those territories.

Katz uses as his starting point a series of lithographs based on drawings that the English architect and illustrator Frederick Catherwood created during two expeditions to the Mayan ruins in the Yucatán peninsula in the 1840s. Catherwood's illustrations, produced with the aid of a camera lucida, were published in two very influential books: *Incidents of Travel in Central America, Chiapas, and Yucatan* (1841) (fig. 3) and *Views of Ancient Monuments in Central America, Chiapas, and Yucatan* (1844), with texts by the American writer and antiquarian John Lloyd Stephens. It was largely through these volumes, today considered paradigmatic of a romanticized vision of the Americas, that Europeans learned of the existence of these ruins, which they would later go on to study in depth.

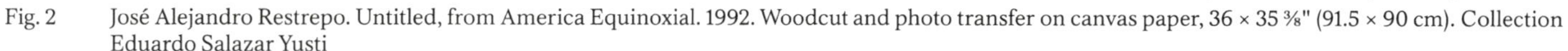

Fig. 2   José Alejandro Restrepo. Untitled, from America Equinoxial. 1992. Woodcut and photo transfer on canvas paper, 36 × 35 ⅜" (91.5 × 90 cm). Collection Eduardo Salazar Yusti

Fig. 3   Frederick Catherwood, illustration of a stone monument in Copán, Honduras, in John Lloyd Stephens, *Incidents of Travel in Central America, Chiapas, and Yucatan*, vol. 1 (London: J. Murray, 1841). The Metropolitan Museum of Art, New York

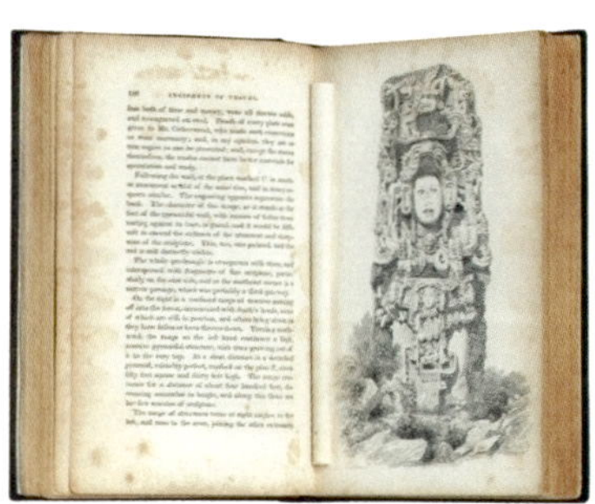

While in Restrepo's *Paso del Quindío I* the chain of references is implicit, Katz addresses Catherwood's lithographs explicitly in most of his photographs, capturing the sites from the exact same perspective used by his predecessor. Some works, like *Arco de Labná, Interior, a la manera de Catherwood* (*Labná's Arch, Interior, after Catherwood*) (1991, plate 6), show the English artist's "original" image alongside Katz's own. Others include only new photographic representations of the monuments, as in *Templo de la Frondosa Cruz, Palenque* (*Temple of the Foliated Cross, Palenque*) (1986, plate 2), where a deliberately dark palette and atmospheric skies enhance the romanticism of the expeditionary gaze contemplating the ruin. In others, such as *Ídolo a medio enterrar, Copán* (*Half-Buried Idol, Copán*)

6   Interview with Restrepo by Turner.

7   To explore the mnemonic function of *Paso del Quindío*, at one presentation the artist installed the work with a massive black-and-white curtain in the background, printed with images of his ascent to the pass superimposed on images of a pile of bodies of people killed during the brutal Colombian Thousand Days' War of 1899–1902 (fig. 2). It was a way of underscoring the traumatic relationship between landscape and violence in Colombia's history. This piece was complemented by *Paso del Quindío II* (1999), which includes the figure of perhaps the last of the *cargueros*, local men who carried travelers on long, difficult journeys.

8   In 2008, the Nigerian curator Okwui Enwezor curated *Archive Fever* (2008), an exhibition that opened the global debate on works that explore archives and dispute the materials they contain. For this show, Enwezor wrote, "Throughout the XIX century, the 'great game' of imperial expansion was an acquisitive game of spatial dominance but one invested with the superior capacity to control the flow of information through the archive." Okwui Enwezor, *Archive Fever: Uses of the Document in Contemporary Art* (New York: International Center of Photography; Göttingen: Steidl, 2008), 21.

(1989, plate 8), *Kabah, Interior, a la manera de Catherwood* (*Kabah, Interior [After Catherwood]*) (1993, plate 13), and *Tulúm, a la manera de Catherwood (El Castillo)* (*Tulúm, after Catherwood [The Castle]*) (1985, plate 5), Katz's process is humorously didactic: he takes the photo from the same vantage point as Catherwood, but includes in the frame his own hand holding the book as source material. These latter images thus feature two representational moments separated by more than a century. And while Katz maintains that "the European eye coins the culture in its own terms," he also acknowledges that, as an Argentine visiting these places for the first time and including his own body in the photographic frame, "I cannot deny my own manipulation of reality."[9] It is for this reason that Katz articulates both representations in his work contiguously, assuming his own perspective as a resonance and as part of a long history of exploration.

A large-scale work by Dominican artist Firelei Báez, part of her series Map Paintings, uses another angle to illuminate the distortions and mystifications generated by the European monopoly on images of America in the early modern period. Here we witness an exercise in prodigious imagination and sumptuous production, in which Báez both underscores and defies the stigmas of the past. In *Untitled (Terra Nova)* (2020, plate 19), she superimposes the image of an extravagant creature onto a canvas printed with one of the earliest maps of the Atlantic Ocean, published in 1541.[10] Part human, part plant, the figure has the body of a Black woman with skin covered in fur; a head of wet, genital-like flesh; and abundantly colored petals surmounted by a lush crown of palm leaves that come together in a headpiece larger than the body itself.

For Báez, maps are historical documents of power, a "projection of desires" by those who drew them.[11] The central figure Báez has painted is based on the Dominican myth of the Ciguapa, a being who encapsulates the idealized image of the Other that inhabits the New World as a lustful monster, a creature beyond human dimensions. Science and myth-making emerge in this work as converging impulses of spatial representation. "What I want to do is transform folklore into a speculative space," says Báez.[12] Poised on the ostensible rationality of the map, the monstrous figure is an explosion of strength and sensuality that highlights the syncretic, transatlantic imaginary and the power of resistant mythologies.

Báez's work comes two decades after that of the South American artists discussed above, and she operates from an identity as a Dominican-American woman living in the United States at a time when the emancipatory discourse over decolonialization has expanded from cultural spaces and objects (as in the examples of Restrepo and Katz) to subaltern bodies.[13] In this context, the ideas of Cameroonian theorist Achille Mbembe about the place of myth-making in the construction of what he calls "Black reason" are useful for interpreting the figure in Báez's painting. As Mbembe discusses in his 2013 book, from the fourteenth to the nineteenth century the Atlantic Ocean was the arena for European expansion and the consolidation of the slave system; as such, it was also the space for fostering concepts of race that created monsters, "caricatures," like the one in Báez's work. Mbembe argues that it was, on the one hand, "the accounts of travelers, explorers,

9   Susana Torruella Leval, "Recapturing History: The (Un)official Story in Contemporary Latin American Art," *Art Journal*, no. 51 (Winter 1992): 69–80.

10   Michael Servetus's *Ptolemy's Geographia*, using Lorenz Fries's woodcut maps, was published by Gaspar Trechsel in Vienna in 1541.

11   Firelei Báez, in a virtual studio visit, May 11, 2022, organized by Elise Chagas as part of the series *Common Ground/Territorio Comun*, Cisneros Institute, The Museum of Modern Art.

12   Báez, virtual studio visit.

13   This focus on bodies is a clue to understanding the importance of figuration in recent art.

soldiers, adventurers, merchants, missionaries, and settlers" and, on the other hand, the "constitution of a 'colonial science'" which mediated and established a figure of the Black person who "stood apart from the normal existence of the human race." This "work of fantasy, . . . when focused on other worlds, constantly blurred the lines between the believable and the unbelievable, the factual and the marvelous."[14] As seen in *Untitled (Terra Nova)*, the concept of the fantastic entails horror as well as fascination.

The genre of landscape has long been a cultural object of primary importance in the exploration, trafficking, and consolidation of European notions of beauty, riches, and the (supposed) virginity of the American territories (lands to be discovered and conquered).[15] Several artists in the exhibition, including the Peruvian Gilda Mantilla and the Colombian Raimond Chaves, who have worked together since 2001, aim to disrupt these perceptions. Their project *Dibujando América* (*Drawing America*), which led them to various parts of Latin America from 2005 to 2008, both performed and questioned the idea of exploration. At one of the many stops on their journey, they visited the collections of magazines, books, and photographs in the Biblioteca Amazónica, part of the Centro de Estudios Teológicos Amazónicos, in Iquitos, Peru. Fascinated by what they found, they returned several years later, drawn by the possibility of undertaking, in their own words, a critical analysis of "how images lead to the symbolic construction of a territory."[16]

Their work *Secretos de la Amazonía* (*Secrets of the Amazon*) (2011, plate 15) uses as its starting point a dissection of the text *Los secretos de la Amazonía: Manual de supervivencia en la selva* (fig. 4), written in 1981 by Peruvian professor César Huamán Ramírez, along with scans of black-and-white photographs from the 1988 book *De Misahuallí a Chaguaramas: en canoa del Amazonas al Caribe* (fig. 5). Made up of two sets of forty slides that simultaneously tell the story of the region's meteorological, anthropological, and cultural conditions, the installation deliberately uses the obsolete pedagogical tool of slide projection to bring out the anachronism of the narrator's voice in Huamán Ramírez's text as he describes "what life is like in places inhabited by semi-civilized, savage people" or "this marvelous, mysterious, spellbinding world, whose countless landscapes of great beauty delight and awaken the curiosity of even those souls most inured to the things of nature." At the same time, the work features blurry black-and-white landscapes to create, as the artists explain, "a kind of anti-landscape theory, so that we may deliberately get lost in the density of the paper, the stains and the signs" of the images that appear alongside the texts.

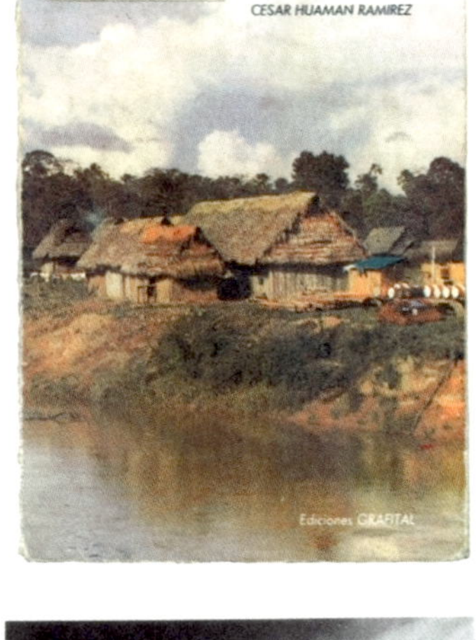

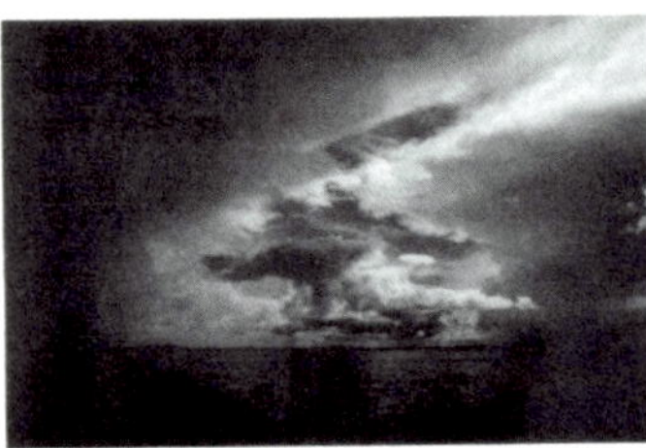
Confluencia del río Tomo en el Orinoco, parque natural del Tomo y Tuparro

Figs. 4, 5   Source material for Gilda Mantilla and Raimond Chaves, *Secretos de la Amazonía*, 2011: César Huamán Ramírez, *Los secretos de la Amazonía: Manual de supervivencia en la selva* (Lima: Grafital Editores, 1981); and photograph from Polidoro Pinto Escobar and Roberto Franco, *De Misahuallí a Chaguaramas: en canoa del Amazonas al Caribe* (Colombia: Instituto Nacional de los Recursos Naturales Renovables y del Medio Ambiente, 1988)

"We took scientific expeditions in America as an unavoidable reference," the artists point out. "Our position as traveling artists could equate us with chroniclers or expeditionists, figures who in their respective moments built and shaped a very significantly accepted American imaginary, as collaborating with an extractive colonial presence. In this sense, we choose to suspend our capacity

14   Achille Mbembe, *Critique of Black Reason* (Durham, N.C.: Duke University Press, 2017), 17.

15   For a discussion of these topics, see Jens Andermann, Lisa Blackmore, and Dayron Carrillo Morell, *Natura: Environmental Aesthetics after Landscape* (Zurich: Diaphanes, 2018).

16   Gilda Mantilla and Raimond Chaves, "Las imágenes propician la construcción de un territorio," *El Español*, February 13, 2019, https://www.elespanol.com/el-cultural/arte/20190213/gilda-mantilla-raimond-chaves-propician-construccion-territorio/375964295_0.html.

of imposing a 'portrait' of a place and rather choose to try open interpretations of what we found, establishing links to other spaces and other times."[17] Given the preponderance of images showcasing the abundance of the Amazon, this work avoids direct visual representation and instead points out the clichés inherent to the ideological construct of the region as an "other" territory. What we see, instead, is a series of grayish, bookish, pointillist images that have banished romanticism and platitudes.

Something similar is at work in the photographs of Venezuelan artist Suwon Lee, who is equally determined to avoid the stereotypes associated with the history of these landscapes. The premise of her series Crepuscular is simple: in each of the pieces in the exhibition—*Lights On*, *Purple Haze*, and *The Most Dangerous City in the World*, all from 2011 (plates 21–23)—Lee reverses the typical perspective seen in landscape paintings and photographs of these same sites. In *Lights On*, she captures her native city of Maracaibo from almost directly above, no small feat given the complexity of the surrounding topography. Rarely photographed from this vantage point, the city appears illuminated, like a shimmering lake of gold. In contrast, the rosy fog of *Purple Haze*, shot from São Paulo's famed modernist Copan Building (which is deliberately absent from the frame), is the optical result of the pollution that hangs over the city. The title of the third image, *The Most Dangerous City in the World*, describes Caracas in the stigmatizing language of statistics. This dark, misty view of the city is captured from El Ávila, a mountain that overlooks Caracas and was made iconic by the history of Venezuelan landscape painting. Lee's images oscillate between her efforts to avoid cliché and to discover a new sublime. As the artist says:

> I drew a lot of inspiration from the Venezuelan Círculo de Bellas Artes painters, who in turn were influenced by the foreign painters and naturalists that came through Venezuela in the eighteenth and nineteenth centuries, figures like Alexander von Humboldt, Anton Goering, and Ferdinand Bellerman. . . . The idea was to explore and rethink the contemporary landscape by positioning myself in unlikely places in order to find . . . a new interpretation of and perspective on those cities.[18]

In their assertion of colonization as the foundational trauma of modernity, the works discussed above function as a point of entry into questions of economics and related debates on dependence and independence—central problems for the art of the region which are, in turn, intimately linked to debates surrounding heritage and patrimony. Originally created in 2010 for the exhibition *On Rage*, at the Haus der Kulturen der Welt in Berlin, Regina José Galindo's *Looting* is a work that portrays mining as extractivism and, as the title suggests, a kind of crime.[19] In the first part of the performance, which took place in her native Guatemala, the artist had eight fillings, made of pure Guatemalan gold, inserted into her molars by

Returns

17   Interview with Gilda Mantilla and Raimond Chaves by Madeline Murphy Turner, May 7, 2020, "Study of the Cisneros Gift."

18   Suwon Lee, quoted in Madeline Murphy Turner, "Landscape and Distance in the Art of Suwon Lee," *MoMA Magazine*, November 11, 2020, https://www.moma.org/magazine/articles/450.

19   The term *extractivism* refers to the intensive exploitation of natural resources for export. For a discussion of this topic, see Maristella Svampa, *Neo-Extractivism in Latin America: Socio-environmental Conflicts, the Territorial Turn, and New Political Narratives* (Cambridge: Cambridge University Press, 2019). For a discussion of mining as the foundational economy of modernity, see Horacio Machado Aráoz, "La minería colonial y las raíces del Capitaloceno: Habitus extractivista y mineralización de la condición humana," *Ambientes* 2, no. 1 (2020): 65–97.

a dentist. In the second part, performed in Germany, she had the fillings removed by another dentist (fig. 6). Galindo describes the symbolic meaning of her piece:

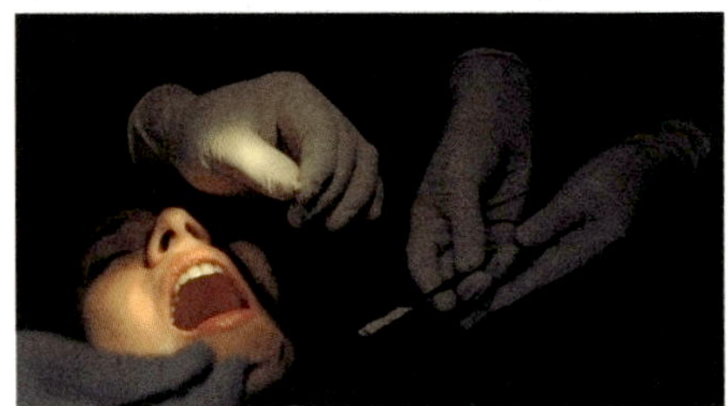

> My mouth represents my country, rich in resources, virgin, immaculate. The drill represents the extraction industry, drilling wantonly, stealing gold without any moral qualms. . . . I always say that history is written mostly on women's bodies—but now I would say it is written on the bodies of those considered to be other. The plunder of life, culture, resources is written in our DNA. We are an eternally looted people, but also a resilient people, a people of struggle and resistance.[20]

Like most of Galindo's works, this piece is a reenactment of an act of violence that is performed at the level of bodily subjection. Yet, in contrast to many of her other works, which take the form of photographic or video documentation of the subjection, only the gold fillings entered MoMA's collection, where they resemble tiny sculptural remnants from a hypothetical archaeological museum (plate 26). The focus is on gold as a natural resource and an object of looting; the space of the body—specifically, the artist's mouth—is not shown but is suggested, by omission, as a territory of extraction and even a means of transport (the artist as mule).

By using her body to shed light on a range of oppressive situations, Galindo brings to the fore ethical questions arising from the representation of suffering. In this sense, a central preoccupation that emerges from her practice—and also applies to other artists in this section—is how to generate emancipatory thinking through repetition (of acts of cruelty, in her case).[21] In *Looting*, that question is not fully resolved but is rather dissolved, through a double absence: the looted territory is left out of the scene and replaced by Galindo's body, which is also not directly or tangibly present. We may perceive it only in the incipient contours of the gold bits, sculpted by the artist's molars like miniature trophies: the result of the looting, museified.

Another work that confronts the centrality of the issue of Latin American economies is *The Fountain of Prosperity (Answers to Some Questions about Bananas)* (2006, plate 28), by the New Zealander Michael Stevenson. This sculpture reproduces the MONIAC, a hydraulic proto-computer that economist A.W.H. Phillips, also from New Zealand, created in 1949 while studying at the London School of Economics (fig. 7). Phillips's goal was to produce a physical model of certain processes of economic flow mapped out by John Maynard Keynes. Unlike other computers of the day, which functioned with perforated cards, the water-based MONIAC had the advantage of showing processes in action, a quality that Phillips considered ideal for educational purposes. The machine, a large panel of tubes, pipes, and containers, was reproduced in the United States, where its champion, the American economist Abba P. Lerner, made a number of adjustments to adapt it to the country's robust economy. This was where it got the nickname "Moniac"—according to Stevenson, a combination of "money" and "maniac," as well as a reference to the ENIAC, one of the first early computers.

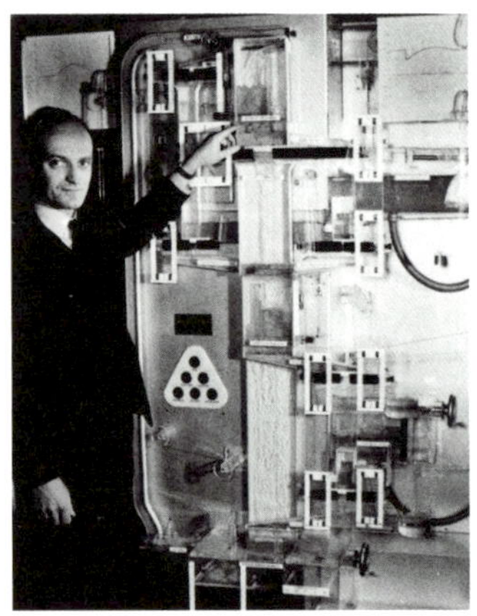

20   Interview with Regina José Galindo by Madeline Murphy Turner (translated by Jane Brodie), April 7, 2020, "Study of the Cisneros Gift." See "On the Violence of the World: A Conversation with Regina José Galindo," *MoMA Magazine*, January 12, 2021, https://www.moma.org/magazine/articles/484.

21   Saidiya Hartman reflects on the trouble with this strategy when speaking of the history of slavery: "What are the protocols and limits that shape the narrative written as counterhistory, an aspiration that isn't a prophylactic against the risks posed by reiterating violent speech and depicting again rituals of torture? How does one revisit the scene of subjection without replicating the grammar of violence?" Saidiya Hartman, "Venus in Two Acts," *Small Axe* 12, no. 2 (2008): 4.

However, what is relevant within the context of Latin America is that, in the early 1950s, the revolutionary government of Guatemalan president Jacobo Arbenz, which had begun a model program of agrarian reform and defied the United Fruit Company's monopoly on the banana industry, also acquired a MONIAC, with more than academic interests in mind. It was purchased for Guatemala's Central Bank, where the machine was to be used to study processes of economic dependence, in the hope that the government might turn around the country's tortured economy and make it prosperous. But shortly thereafter, in 1954, a US-backed coup d'état overthrew Arbenz, and the eccentric apparatus was donated to the Universidad de San Carlos, where, according to Stevenson's research, it disappeared.

What held Stevenson's continued interest in this story was the trust that the Guatemalan establishment had placed in the machine. "It is often the case with complex machines," he says, "that we attribute mysterious powers to them, powers they simply cannot possess. It might turn out to be that Moniac—whose economic capacities were impaired—functioned more as a talismanic adviser on the economy and perhaps even the state. With the enforced regime change in 1954, the machine—and everything it stood for—was cast out."[22] In Stevenson's view, the MONIAC represents an almost mystical belief in the source of prosperity and the resulting failures of developmentalism.

Similar tensions between the promises of modernity and the realities of the present underlie the design of Brasília, the capital of Brazil. The city's ambitious master plan, conceived by Lúcio Costa and Oscar Niemeyer in 1956, radically reconfigured the area where it was implemented in an effort to represent, through geometry as a symbol of order, the dreams of modernization in a complex country marked by inequality. In photographs taken by Hungarian-born Brazilian photographer Thomaz Farkas during the inauguration festivities for Brasília in 1960, one can already see the image of the citizenry destabilizing the project's balanced composition (figs. 8, 9). As São Paulo–based photographer Mauro Restiffe recalls, he traveled to Brasília for the first time in 2003 with the goal of photographing a space that had become iconic, fixed in its own idealizing geometry.[23] Restiffe's time in the city, however, coincided with celebrations of the presidential inauguration of Luiz Inácio Lula da Silva of the Workers' Party, an event that considerably altered the country's political landscape.[24]

Fig. 8, 9   Thomaz Farkas. *People on the Roof of the National Congress, Inauguration of Brasília, April 1960* and *Núcleo Bandeirante*. 1960. Gelatin silver prints, 9 ⁷⁄₁₆ × 14 ³⁄₁₆" (24 × 36 cm). Instituto Moreira Salles

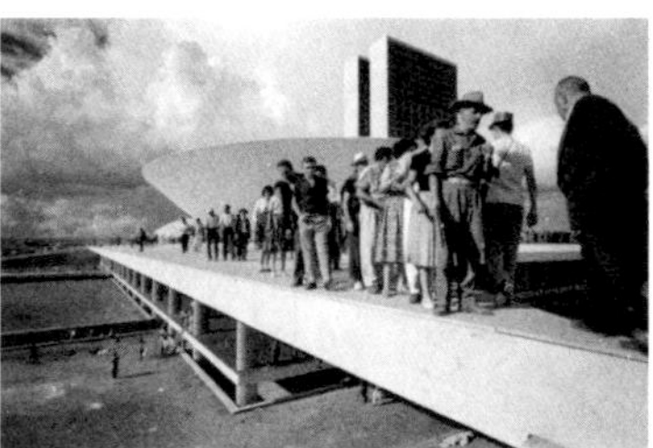

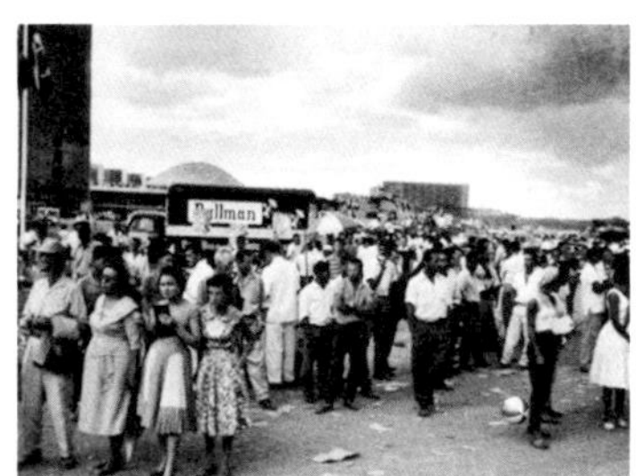

Two black-and-white photographs by Restiffe (plates 24, 25) show crowds celebrating along the Esplanade of the Ministries (*Empossamento #9*, 2003), and a few stragglers wandering through the same space, later littered with papers and other remains of the festivities (*Empossamento #8*, 2003). Both images ignore the charismatic focus of the event and the monumental axis of the city, concentrating instead on the social vibrations generated by the arrival of the new president. The first photograph is taken from what seems to be a small hill or bleachers, as the public cheers on the acrobatics of a group of airplanes that appear as tiny dots in the sky. The energy of the masses emanates from the foreground toward the background of the photo, where people are clustered up close to the perfectly mathematical sequence of Niemeyer's buildings. The air is slightly smoky from

22   Michael Stevenson, "The Search for the Fountain of Prosperity," in *c/o The Central Bank of Guatemala* (San Francisco: CCA Wattis Institute for Contemporary Arts, 2006), n.p.

23   Interview with Mauro Restiffe by Madeline Murphy Turner, August 13, 2020, "Study of the Cisneros Gift."

24   On January 1, 2003, the Spanish newspaper *El País* described the general atmosphere: "Brasilia, the capital designed forty-two years ago by Oscar Niemeyer, has awakened today to a scene of balloons, flags, and travelers from every region of the country, a multitude that has swelled to some 500,000 people. Despite the predictions of rain, only the five-time world champion national football team, the pope, and the deceased former Formula I driver Ayrton Senna have summoned the kind of crowd that Lula has commanded." Translation by Kristina Cordero.

23

the pyrotechnics and the general hubbub. The second photograph documents the same space, but with greater atmospheric definition.

The black and white of the images produces a kind of ambiguous temporality.[25] "Before" and "after" are defined less in relation to the moment of the inauguration and more as a juxtaposition between the historical past, with its projections of order and progress, and a political present that embodies new dreams and disrupts history. Here the landscape produced by the effervescent crowd is understood not as entropy or decadence but rather as life-affirming transformation, and the tension between the monolithic order of the architecture and the intensity of the populace becomes political as well as poetic.

Issues of continuity with longstanding traditions that are central to the second section of the exhibition begin to emerge here. Recent decolonial and feminist reconsiderations of history have inspired contemporary artists to research and radically reassess the textile traditions of the continent, and two pieces in the exhibition connect these legacies with present-day economic and digital networks. The tapestries of the Argentine-born, Los Angeles–based Analia Saban (fig. 10, plate 27), woven with linen and copper threads, intertwine the history of weaving with the history of computers. In each work in the series, the design of a graphics card—in the case of the MoMA piece, the ATI Radeon HD 5970, from 2009 (fig. 11)—is reproduced on a loom. By acknowledging the manual origins of digital technology and contesting the notion of a technological leap by revealing its continuities, these works embody the notion of "seeds of the future that sprout from the depths of the past,"[26] as sociologist Silvia Rivera Cusicanqui described the Aymara conception of history as a spiral rather than linear movement through time.

Fig. 10 Copper tapestry in production in Analia Saban's studio, Los Angeles

Fig. 11 ATI Radeon HD 5970 graphics card

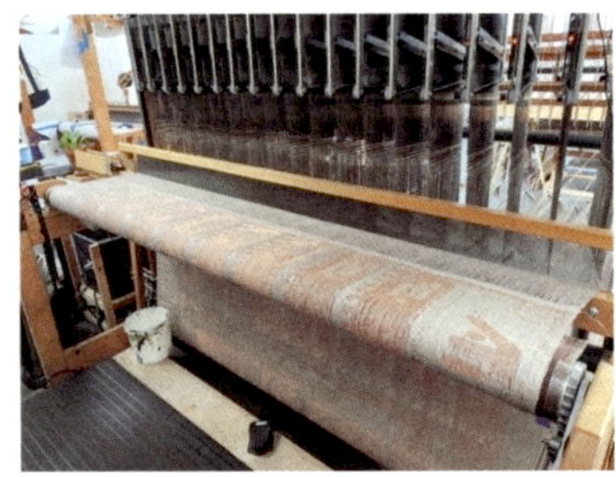

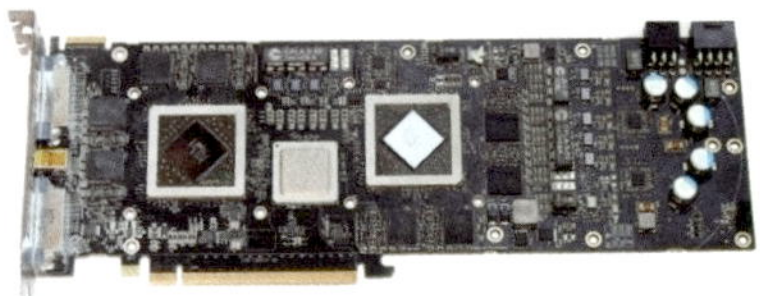

Mexican artist Gabriel Kuri makes a similar connection between weaving and digitalization in *Superama II* (2005), a large-scale reproduction of a supermarket receipt woven on a loom in a Guadalajara workshop (plate 29). And though Kuri denies that he is producing what he refers to as "homespun conceptualism," he admits to an interest in creating bridges between the pre- and post-global worlds. The present-day forms of the market and consumerism are entwined—literally woven together—with a technique that the artist positions as part of another historical paradigm.

Also interested in a critical rereading of modernity, artist Armando Andrade Tudela seeks to question and broaden the modern canon through an investigation of contemporary Andean popular culture. His *Camión* (*Truck*) (2003, plates 36–38) consists of a series of images of trucks, presented as a slide show, whose exteriors feature large geometric designs painted by their owners. The photographs, taken from a moving car on Peruvian highways, point to the ubiquity of a kind of amateur geometric design reminiscent of the American hard-edge work of Ellsworth Kelly, Kenneth Noland, and Frank Stella. But in this case one senses that the designs are rooted in the region's strong geometric textile tradition, which the Argentine artist César Paternosto has discussed as an unacknowledged influence on modern abstraction.[27] Alluding to John Baldessari's self-consciously banal slide work *The Back of All the Trucks Passed While Driving from Los Angeles to Santa Barbara, Calif., Sunday 20 Jan. 63* (1963), Andrade Tudela uncovers, in his travels through Peru, an unexpected modernity.

25 "What interests me," the artist says, is "the timeless aspect of it, the fact that you can barely tell when they were taken." Interview with Restiffe by Turner. This was the first of a series of journeys that Restiffe undertook to attend what he calls "single events": Obama's inauguration in the U.S., the funerals of Niemeyer and Fidel Castro, and Bolsonaro's inauguration in Brazil. These last series were exhibited at the 2021 São Paulo Biennial as a counterpoint to those of Lula's inauguration.

26 Silvia Rivera Cusicanqui, *Ch´ixinakax utxiwa: Una reflexión sobre prácticas y discursos descolonizadores* (Buenos Aires: Tinta Limón, 2010), 55.

27 César Paternosto, *La irrupción del otro: la abstracción en la modernidad tardía* (Heras, Spain: Ediciones La Bahía, 2020).

24

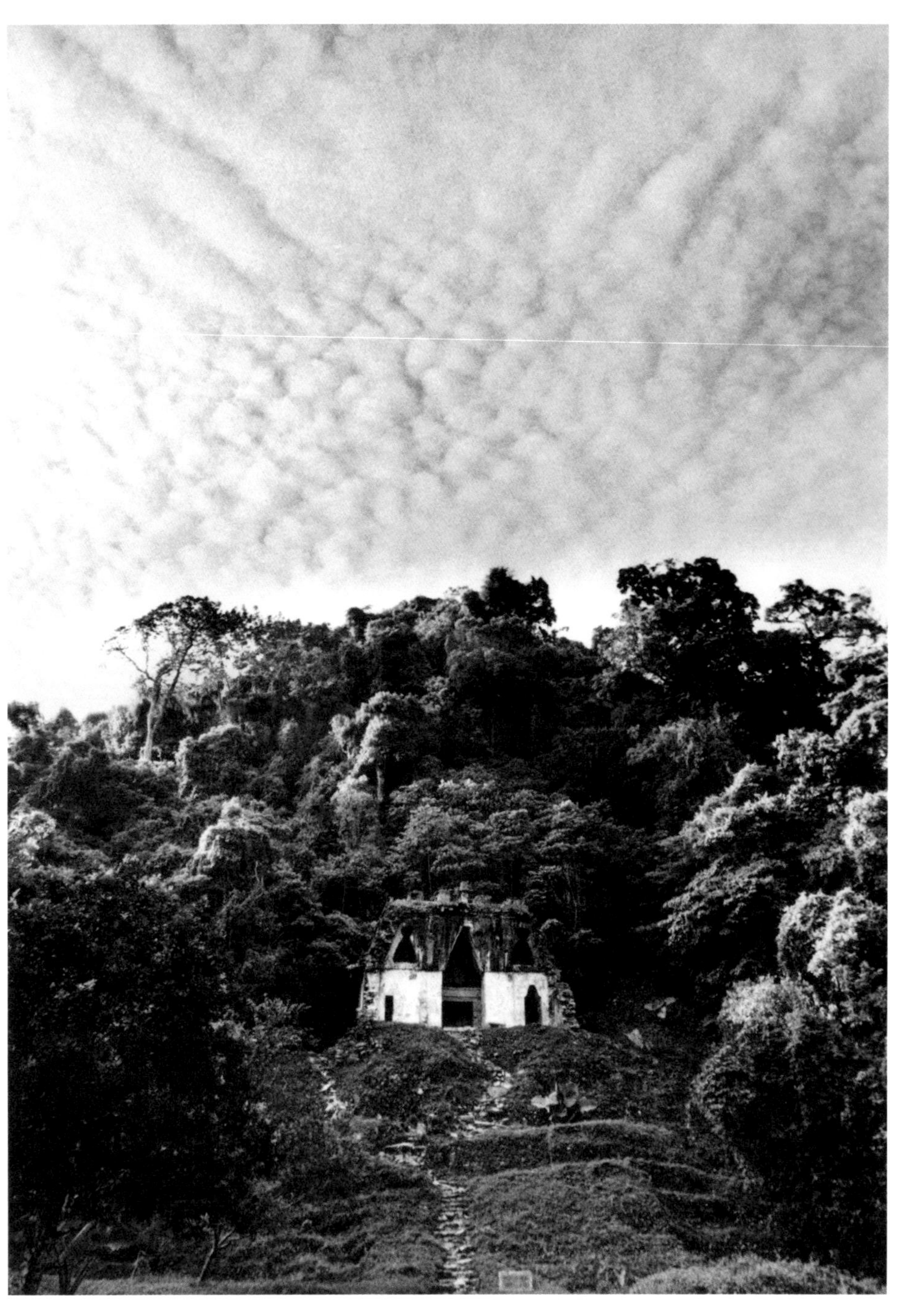

Plate 2

Leandro Katz (Argentine, born 1938)
Templo de la Frondosa Cruz, Palenque (*Temple of the Foliated Cross, Palenque*), from The Catherwood Project. 1986
Gelatin silver print
20 × 16" (50.8 × 40.6 cm)

25

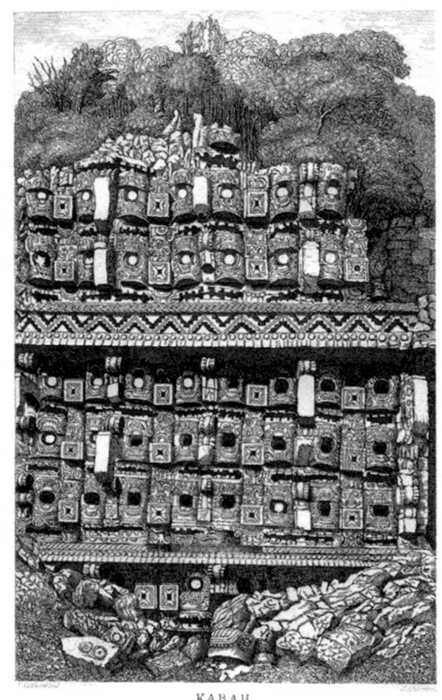

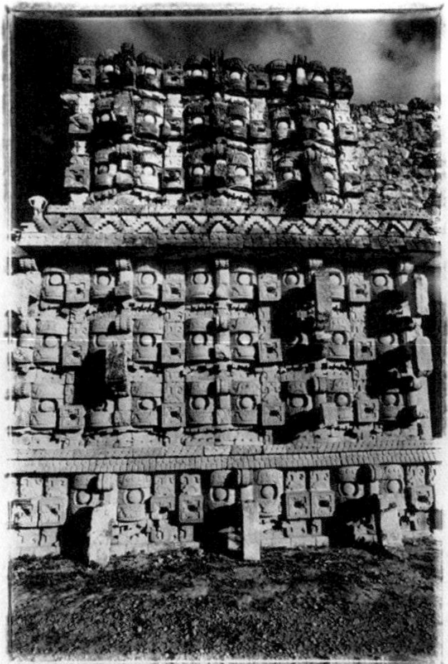

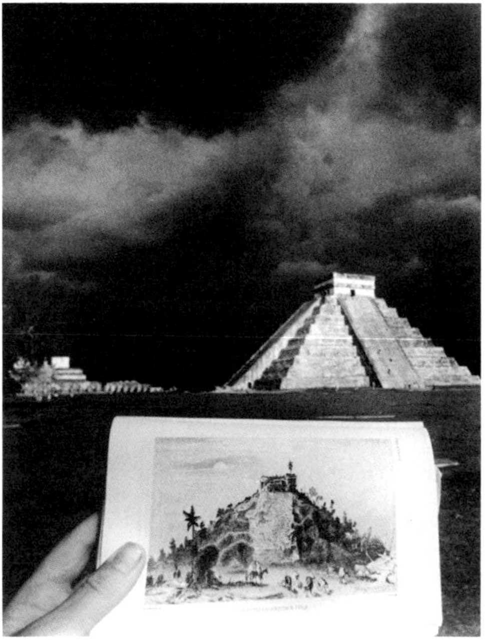

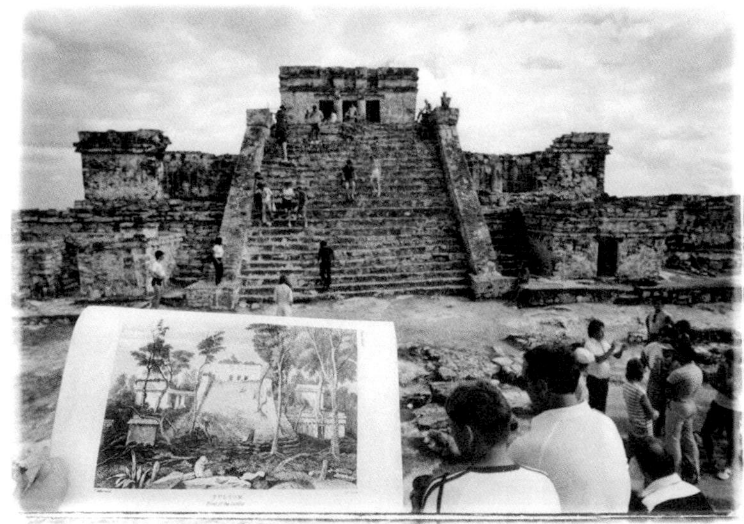

Plate 3   Leandro Katz (Argentine, born 1938)
Kabah, a la manera de Catherwood (Templo de las Máscaras) (*Kabah, after Catherwood [Temple of the Masks]*), from The Catherwood Project. 1985
Gelatin silver print
16 × 20" (40.6 × 50.8 cm)

Plate 4   Leandro Katz (Argentine, born 1938)
El Castillo (Chichén Itzá) (*The Castle [Chichén Itzá]*), from The Catherwood Project. 1985
Gelatin silver print
20 × 16" (50.8 × 40.6 cm)

Plate 5   Leandro Katz (Argentine, born 1938)
Tulúm, a la manera de Catherwood (El Castillo) (*Tulúm, after Catherwood [The Castle]*), from The Catherwood Project. 1985
Gelatin silver print
16 × 20" (40.6 × 50.8 cm)

27

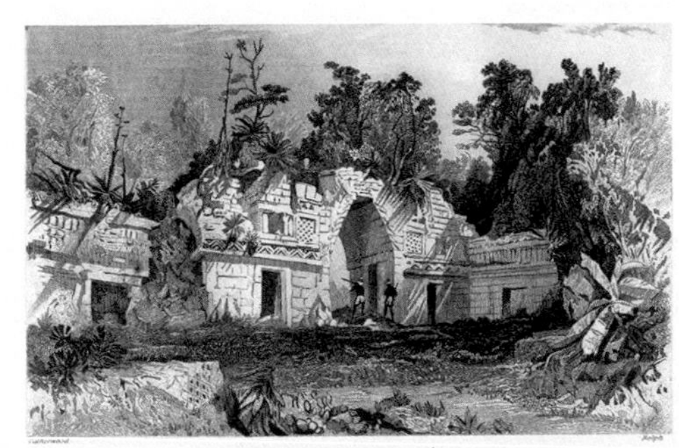

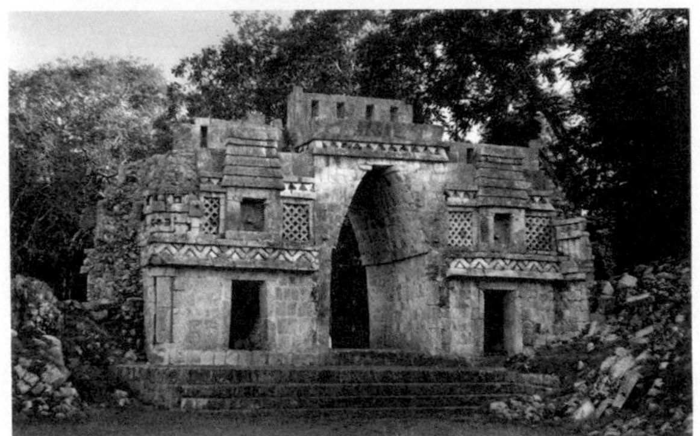

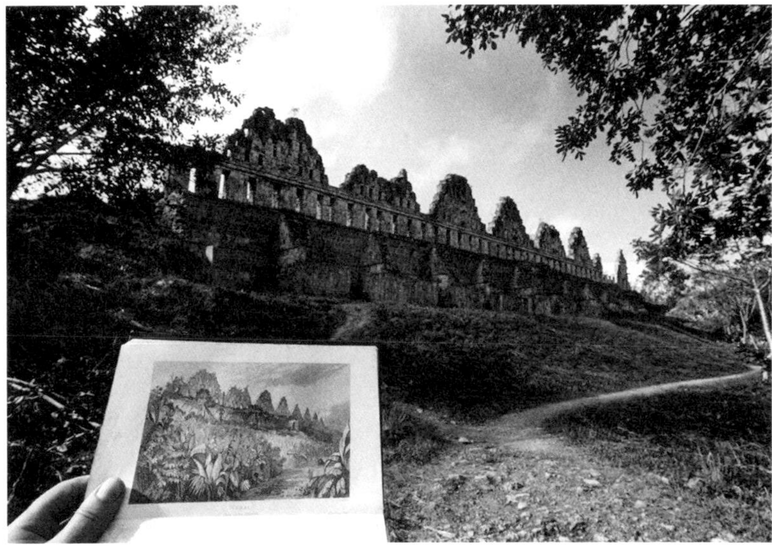

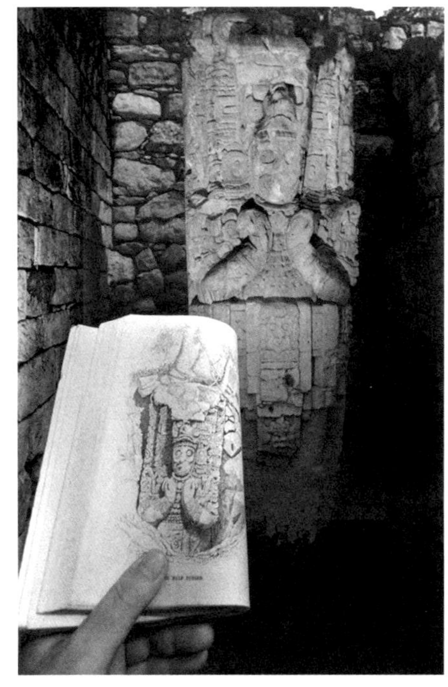

Plate 6 — Leandro Katz (Argentine, born 1938)
Arco de Labná, Interior, a la manera de Catherwood (*Labná's Arch, Interior, after Catherwood*), from The Catherwood Project. 1991
Gelatin silver print
20 × 16" (50.8 × 40.6 cm)

Plate 7 — Leandro Katz (Argentine, born 1938)
Uxmal, Casa de las Palomas (*Uxmal, House of the Doves*), from The Catherwood Project. 1993
Gelatin silver print
16 × 20" (40.6 × 50.8 cm)

Plate 8 — Leandro Katz (Argentine, born 1938)
Ídolo a medio enterrar, Copán (*Half-Buried Idol, Copán*), from The Catherwood Project. 1989
Gelatin silver print
20 × 16" (50.8 × 40.6 cm)

29

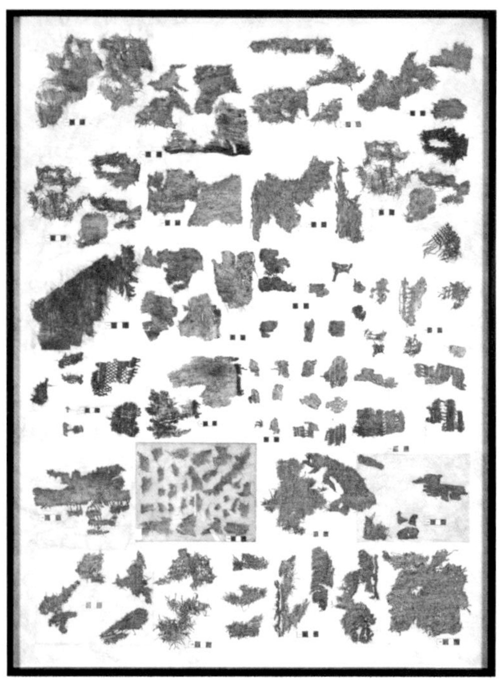

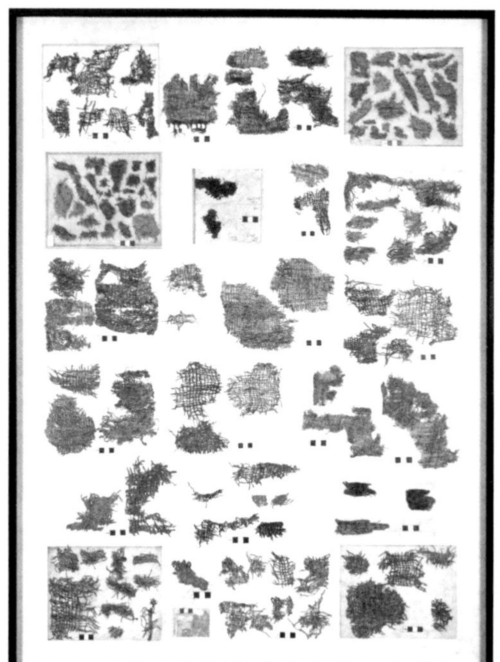

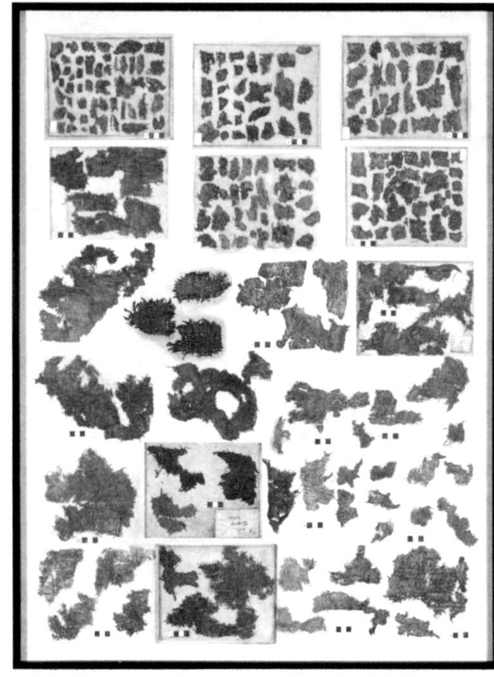

Plate 9

Gala Porras-Kim (Colombian-Korean, born 1984)
124 Offerings for the Rain at the Peabody Museum. 2021
Graphite and ink on paper
46 ⅞ × 35 ⁷⁄₁₆" (119 × 90 cm)

Plate 10

Gala Porras-Kim (Colombian-Korean, born 1984)
122 Offerings for the Rain at the Peabody Museum. 2021
Graphite and ink on paper
46 ⅞ × 35 ⁷⁄₁₆" (119 × 90 cm)

Plate 11

Gala Porras-Kim (Colombian-Korean, born 1984)
203 Offerings for the Rain at the Peabody Museum. 2021
Graphite and ink on paper
46 ⅞ × 35 ⁷⁄₁₆" (119 × 90 cm)

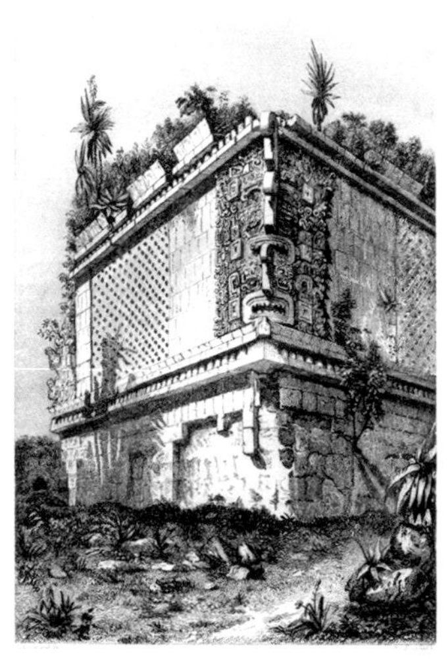

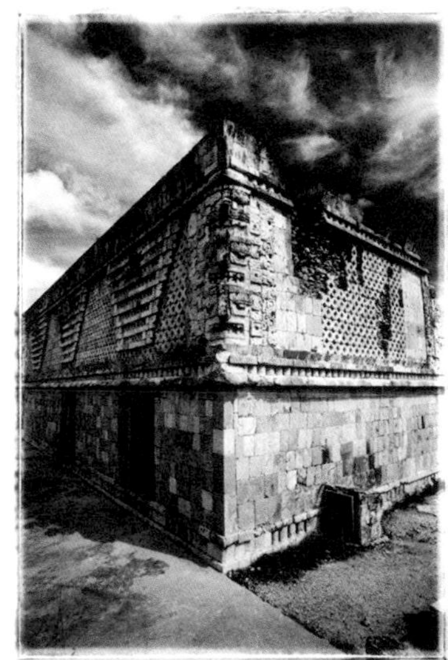

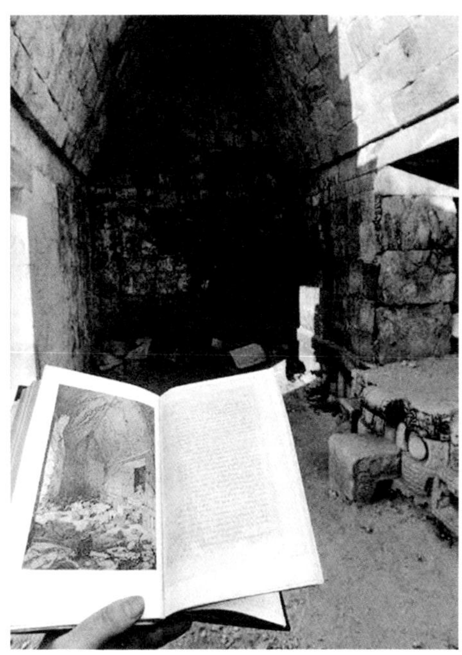

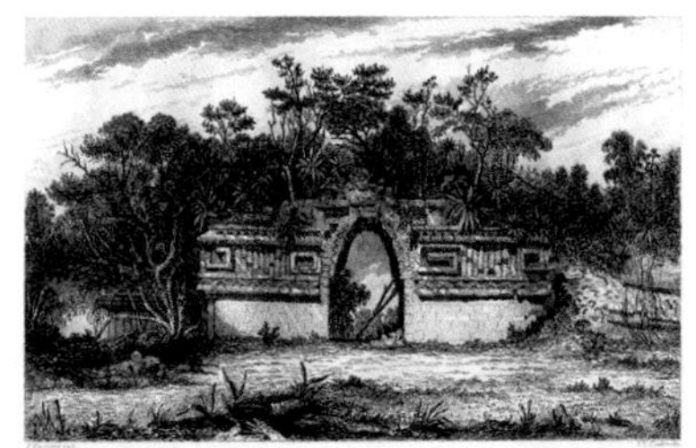

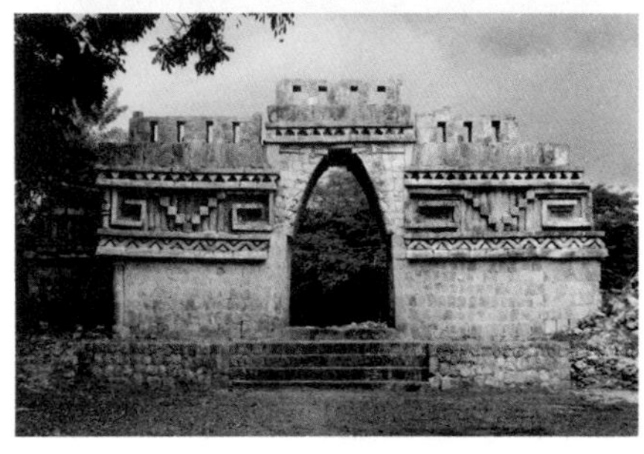

Plate 12

Leandro Katz (Argentine, born 1938)
Uxmal, a la manera de Catherwood (Casa de la Monjas, esq. sureste)
(*Uxmal, after Catherwood [House of the Nuns, Southeast Corner]*),
from The Catherwood Project. 1985
Gelatin silver print
16 × 20" (40.6 × 50.8 cm)

Plate 13

Leandro Katz (Argentine, born 1938)
Kabah, Interior, a la manera de Catherwood (*Kabah, Interior [After
Catherwood]*), from The Catherwood Project. 1993
Gelatin silver print
20 × 16" (50.8 × 40.6 cm)

Plate 14

Leandro Katz (Argentine, born 1938)
Arco de Labná, a la manera de Catherwood (fachada del este) (*Labná's
Arch, after Catherwood [East Facade]*), from The Catherwood Project. 1991
Gelatin silver print
20 × 16" (50.8 × 40.6 cm)

I

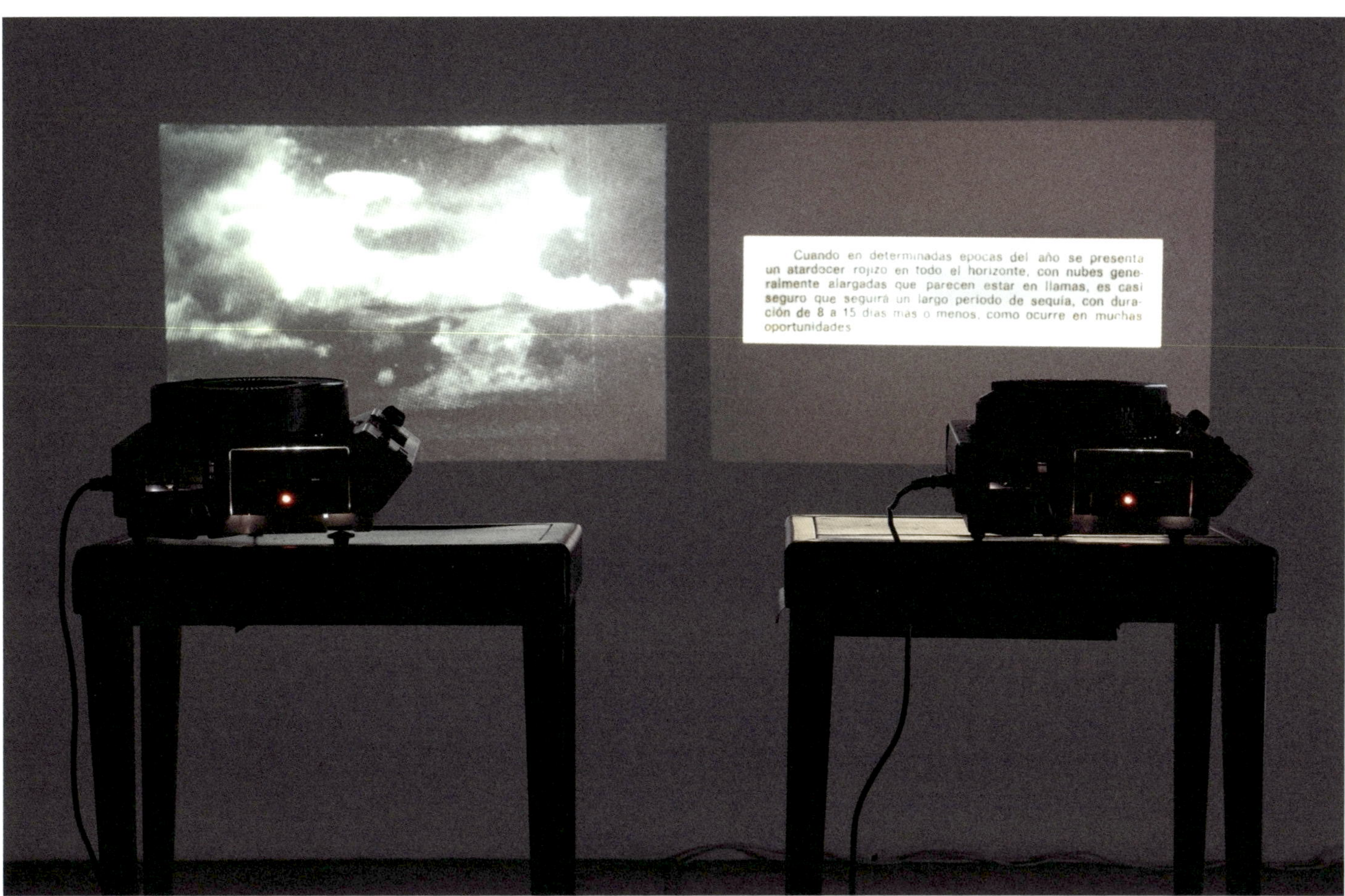

Plate 15

Gilda Mantilla (Peruvian, born United States 1967)
and Raimond Chaves (Colombian, born 1963)
Secretos de la Amazonía (*Secrets of the Amazon*). 2011
Two sets of forty 35mm black-and-white slides

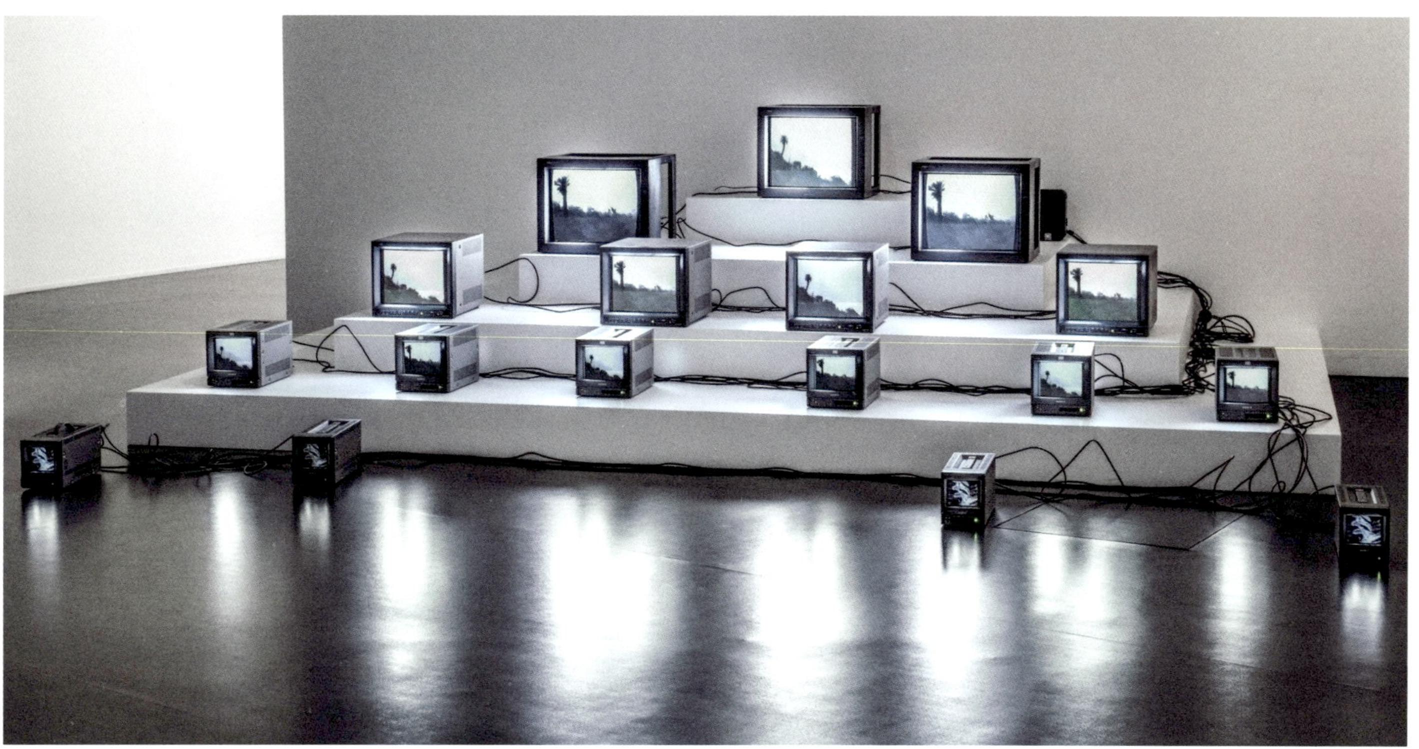

Plate 16

José Alejandro Restrepo (Colombian, born 1959)
Paso del Quindío I (Quindío Pass I). 1992
Three-channel video (black and white, sound, 30 min.) on seventeen
cathode-ray-tube monitors
Dimensions variable

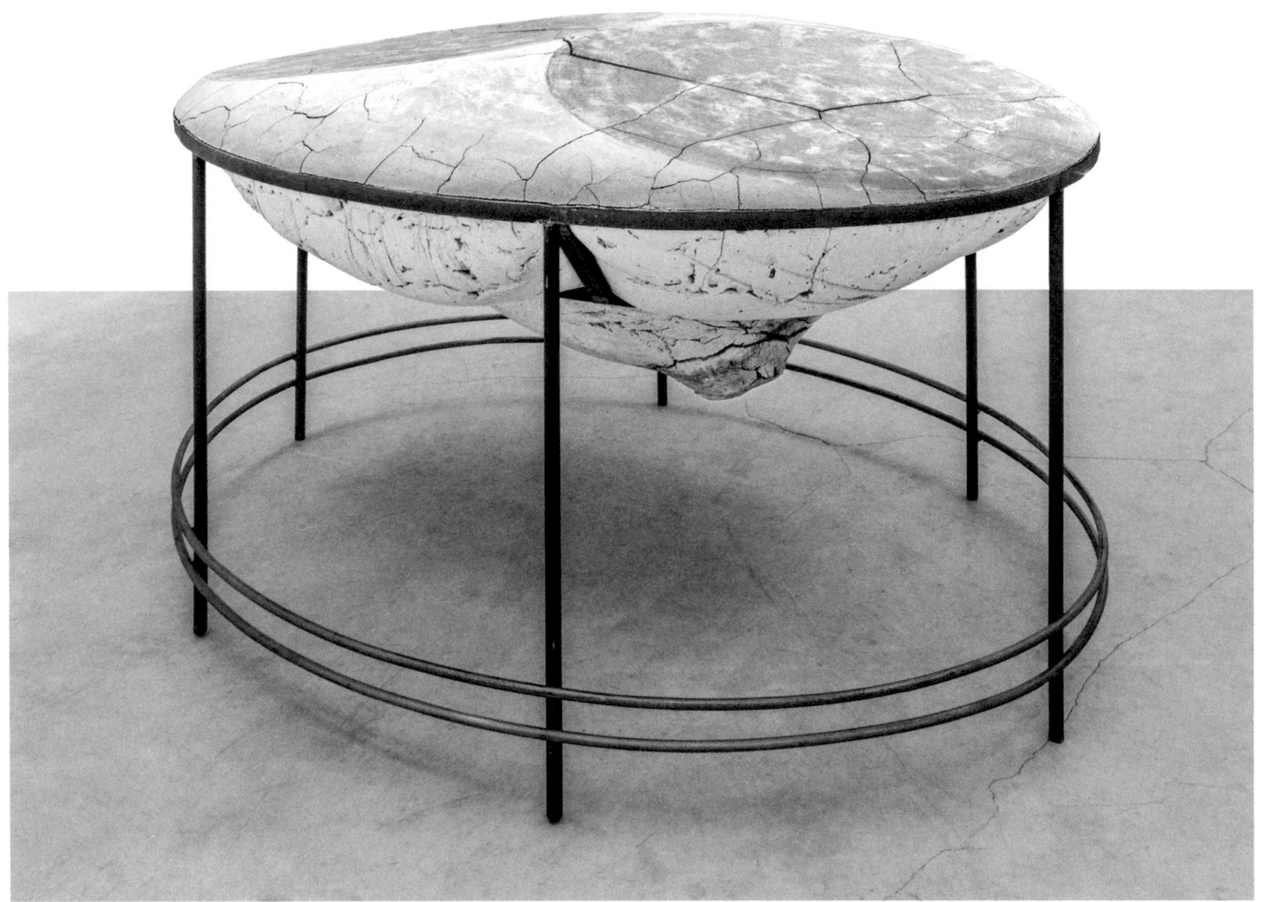

Plate 17

Adrián Villar Rojas (Argentine, born 1980)
Untitled, from Los Teatros de Saturno
(The Theaters of Saturn). 2014
Iron, gesso, and clay
34 ⁷⁄₁₆ × 61 ¹³⁄₁₆ × 46 ⁷⁄₁₆" (87.5 × 157 × 118 cm)
Colección Patricia Phelps de Cisneros

36

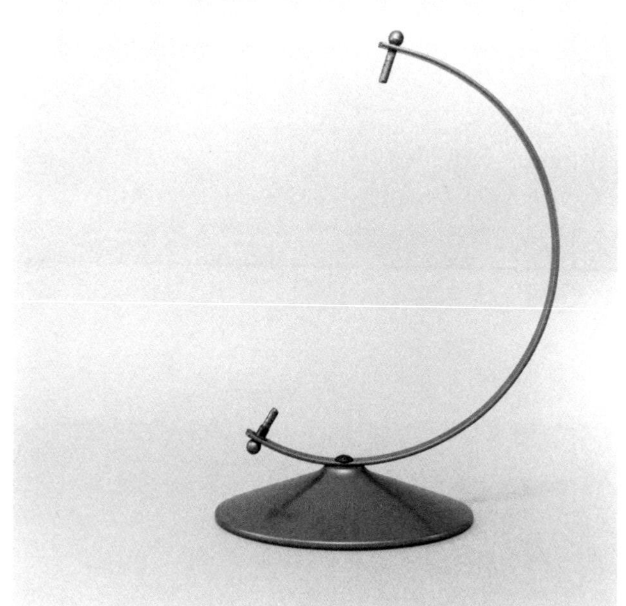

Plate 18

Claudio Perna (Venezuelan, born Italy. 1938–1997)
Untitled. 1990
Gelatin silver print
11 ¼ × 11 ¼" (28.5 × 28.5 cm)

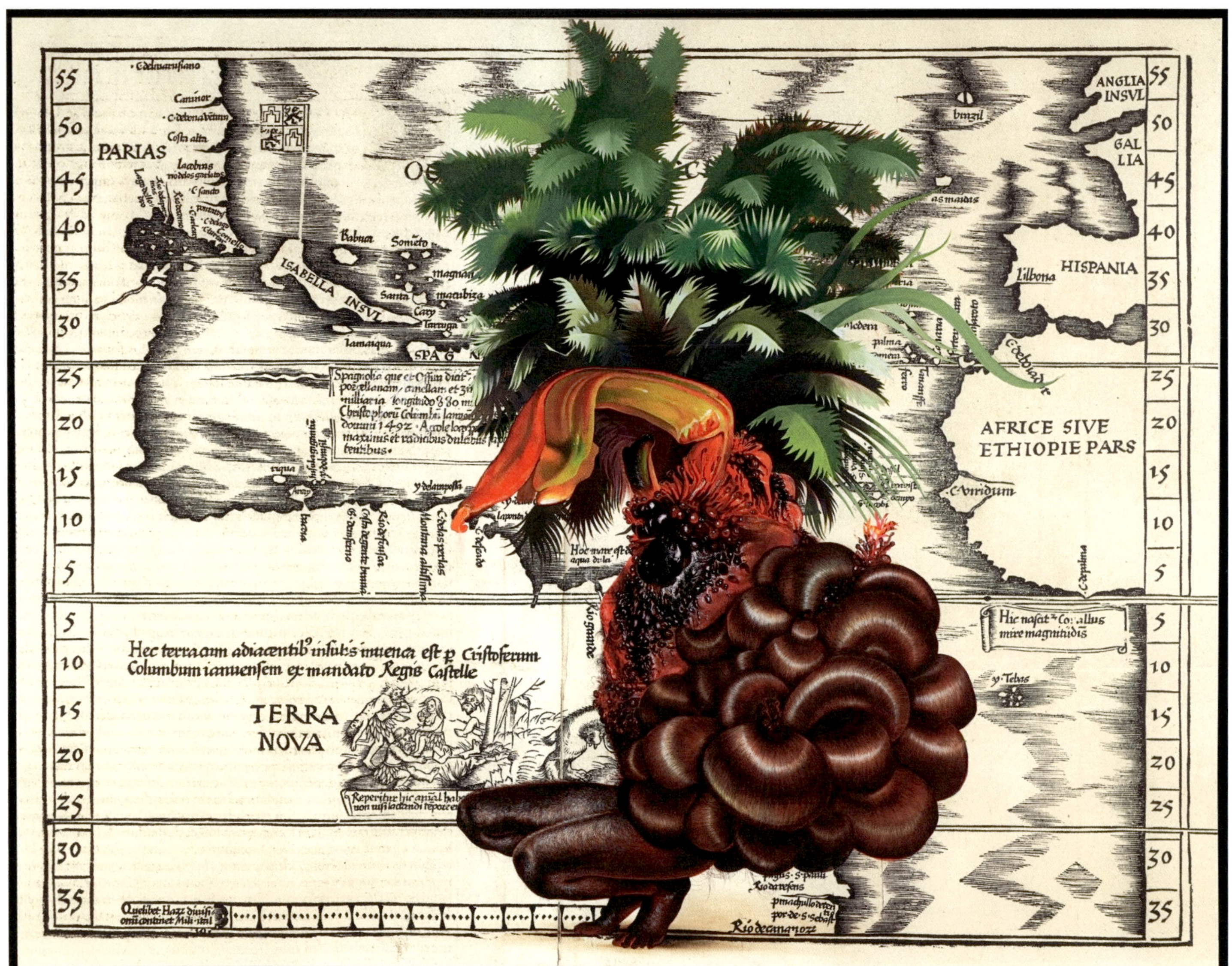

Firelei Báez (Dominican, born 1981)
Untitled (Terra Nova). 2020
Oil and acrylic paint, laser print on canvas
102 ¹³⁄₁₆ × 132 ⁵⁄₁₆ × 1 ⁹⁄₁₆" (261.1 × 336.1 × 4 cm)
Montreal Museum of Fine Arts

38

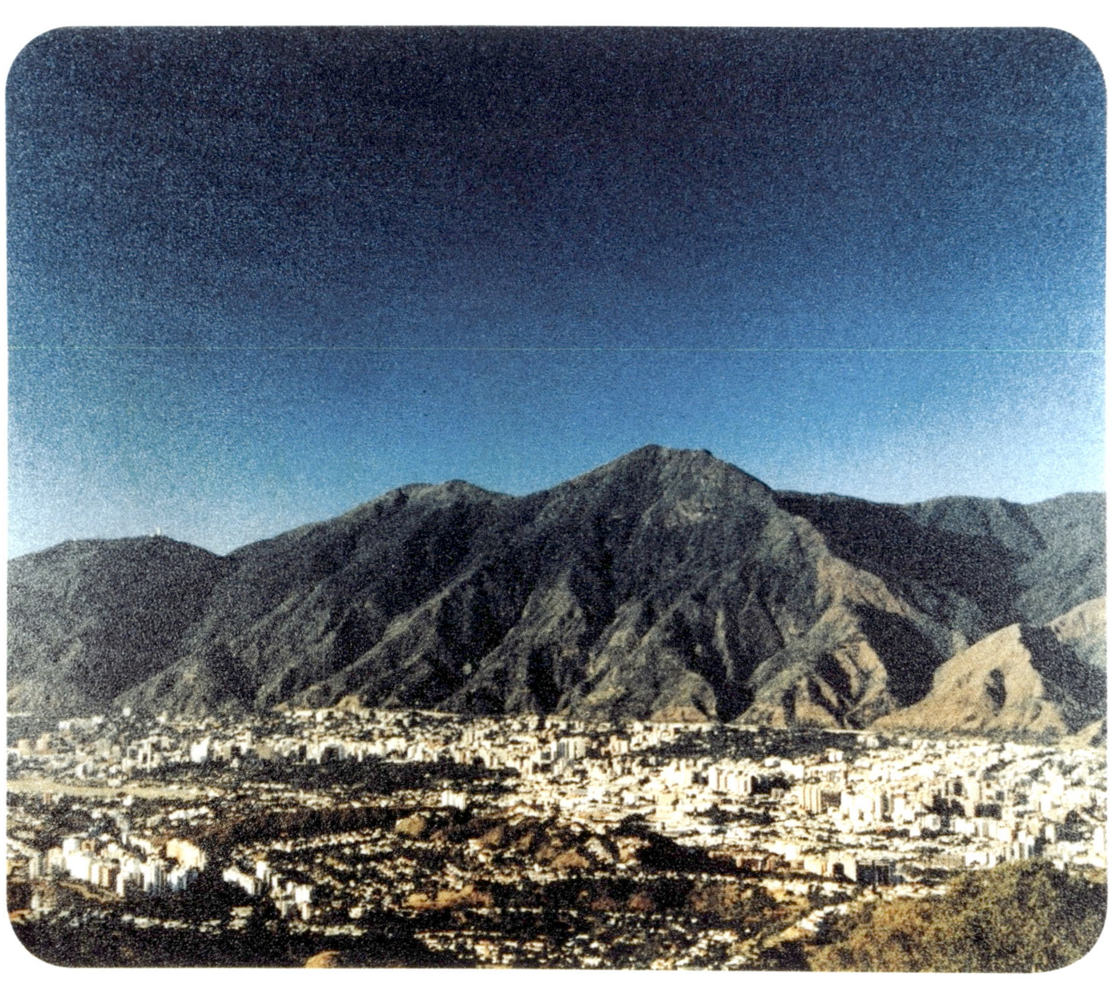

Luis Molina-Pantin (Venezuelan, born Switzerland 1969)
Mouse Pad, from Nuevos paisajes (New Landscapes). 1999–2000
Silver dye bleach print
53 1/8 × 64 15/16" (135 × 165 cm)

39

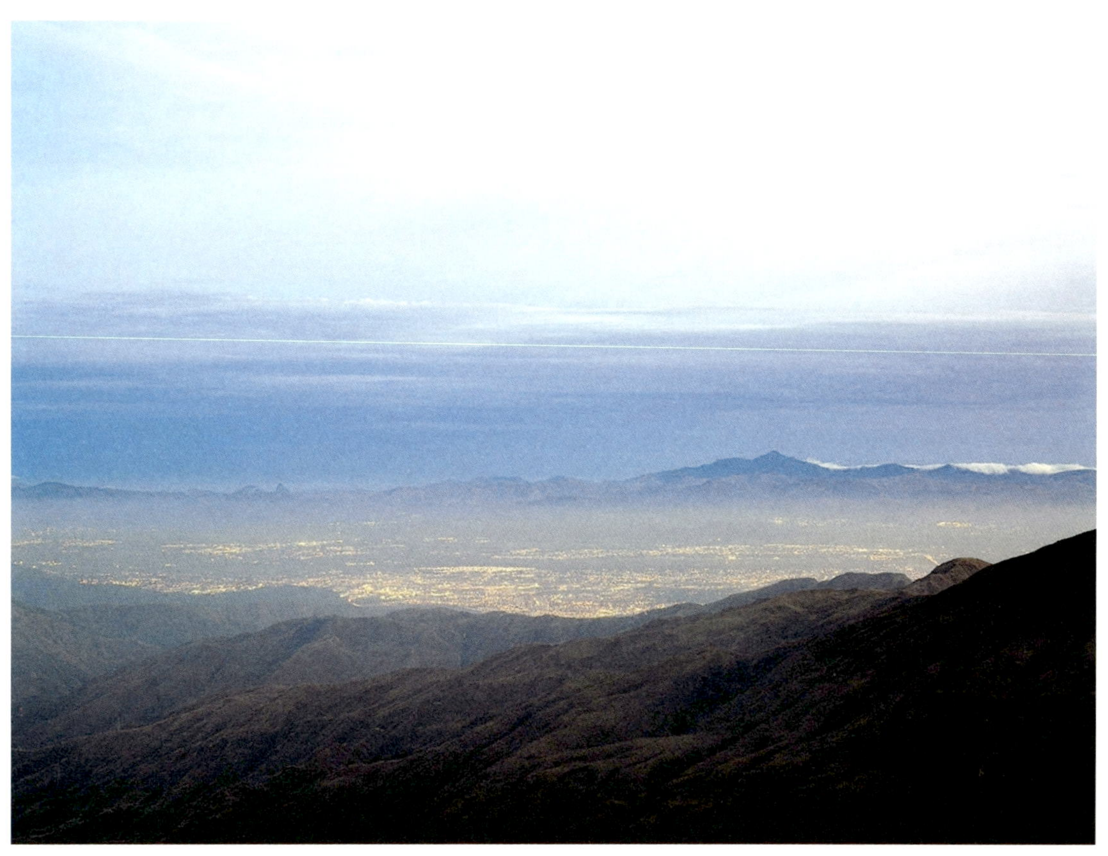

Plate 21

Suwon Lee (Venezuelan, born 1977)
Lights On. 2011
Inkjet print
36 ¼ × 47 ¼" (92 × 120 cm)

41

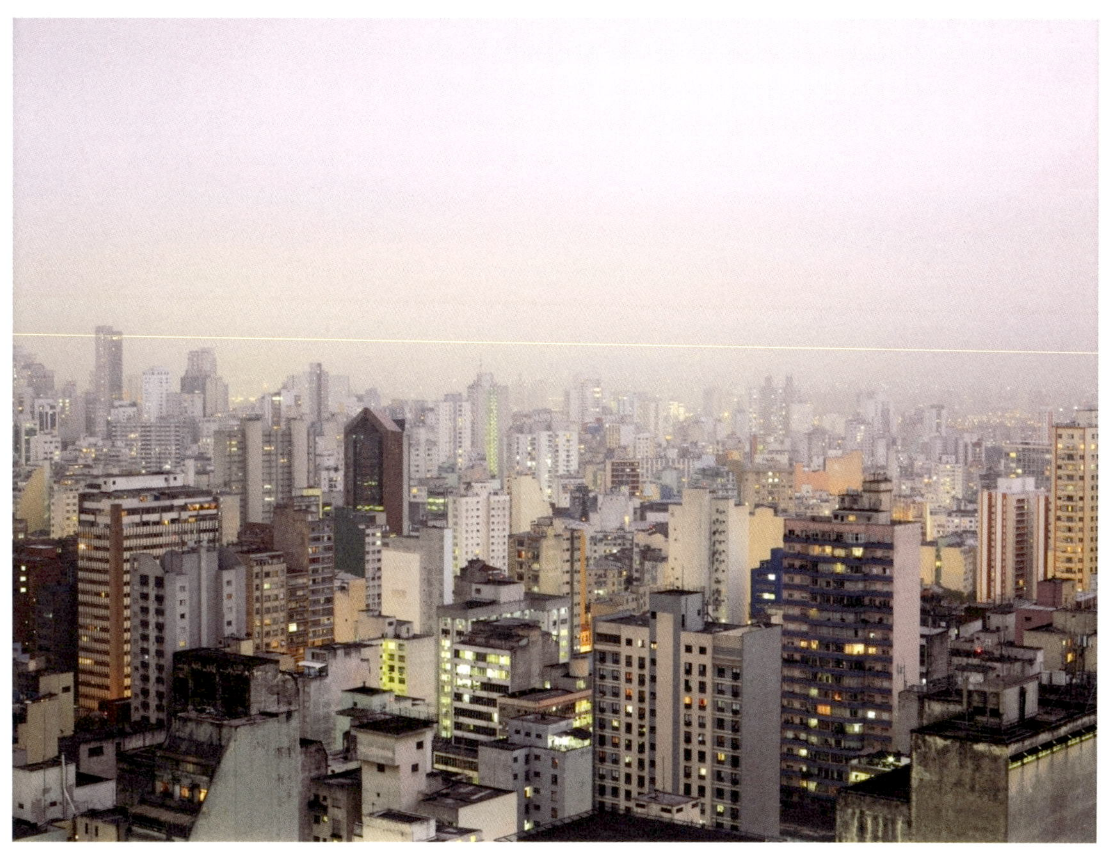

Plate 22

Suwon Lee (Venezuelan, born 1977)
Purple Haze. 2011
Inkjet print
36 ¼ × 47 ¼" (92 × 120 cm)

43

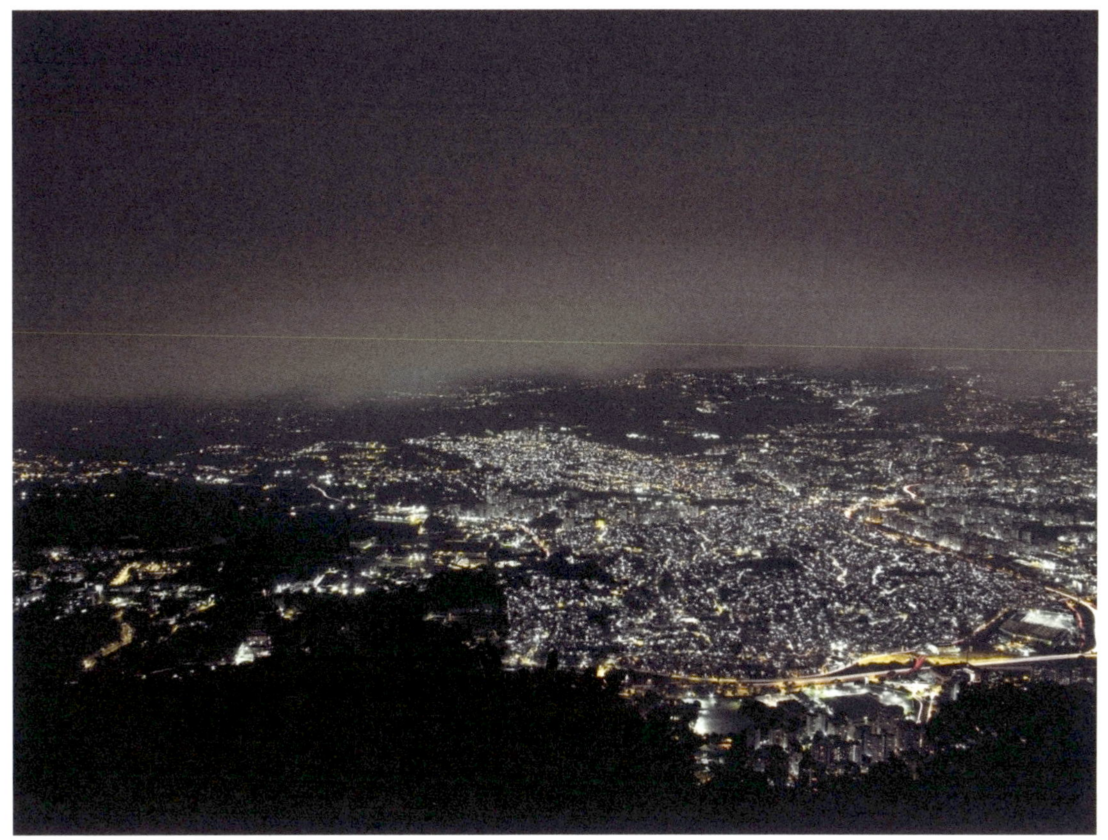

Suwon Lee (Venezuelan, born 1977)
La ciudad más peligrosa del mundo (*The Most Dangerous City in the World*). 2011
Inkjet print
36 ¼ × 47 ⅛" (92.1 × 119.7 cm)

45

I

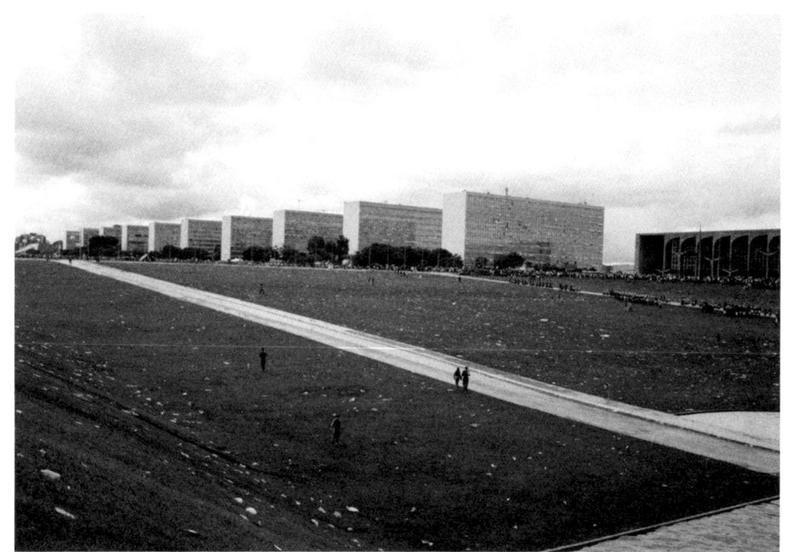

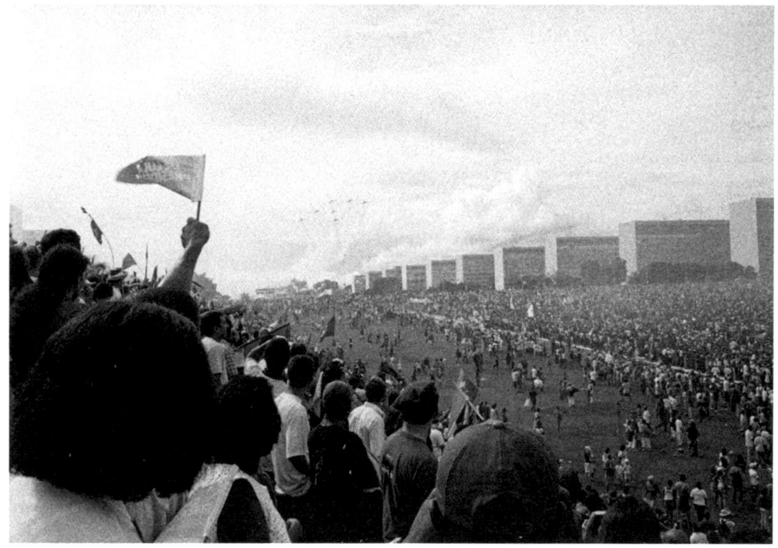

Plate 24

Mauro Restiffe (Brazilian, born 1970)
Empossamento #8 (*Inauguration No. 8*). 2003
Gelatin silver print
14 ½ × 22" (36.8 × 55.9 cm)

Plate 25

Mauro Restiffe (Brazilian, born 1970)
Empossamento #9 (*Inauguration No. 9*). 2003
Gelatin silver print
14 ½ × 22" (36.8 × 55.9 cm)

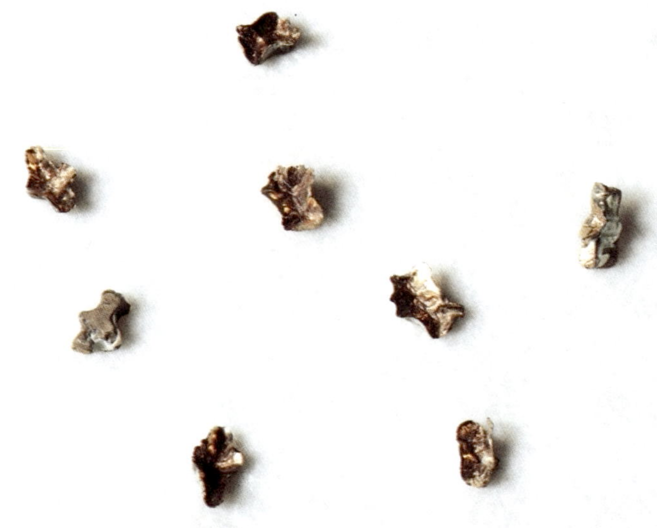

Plate 26

Regina José Galindo (Guatemalan, born 1974)
Looting. 2010
Eight gold fillings
Dimensions variable

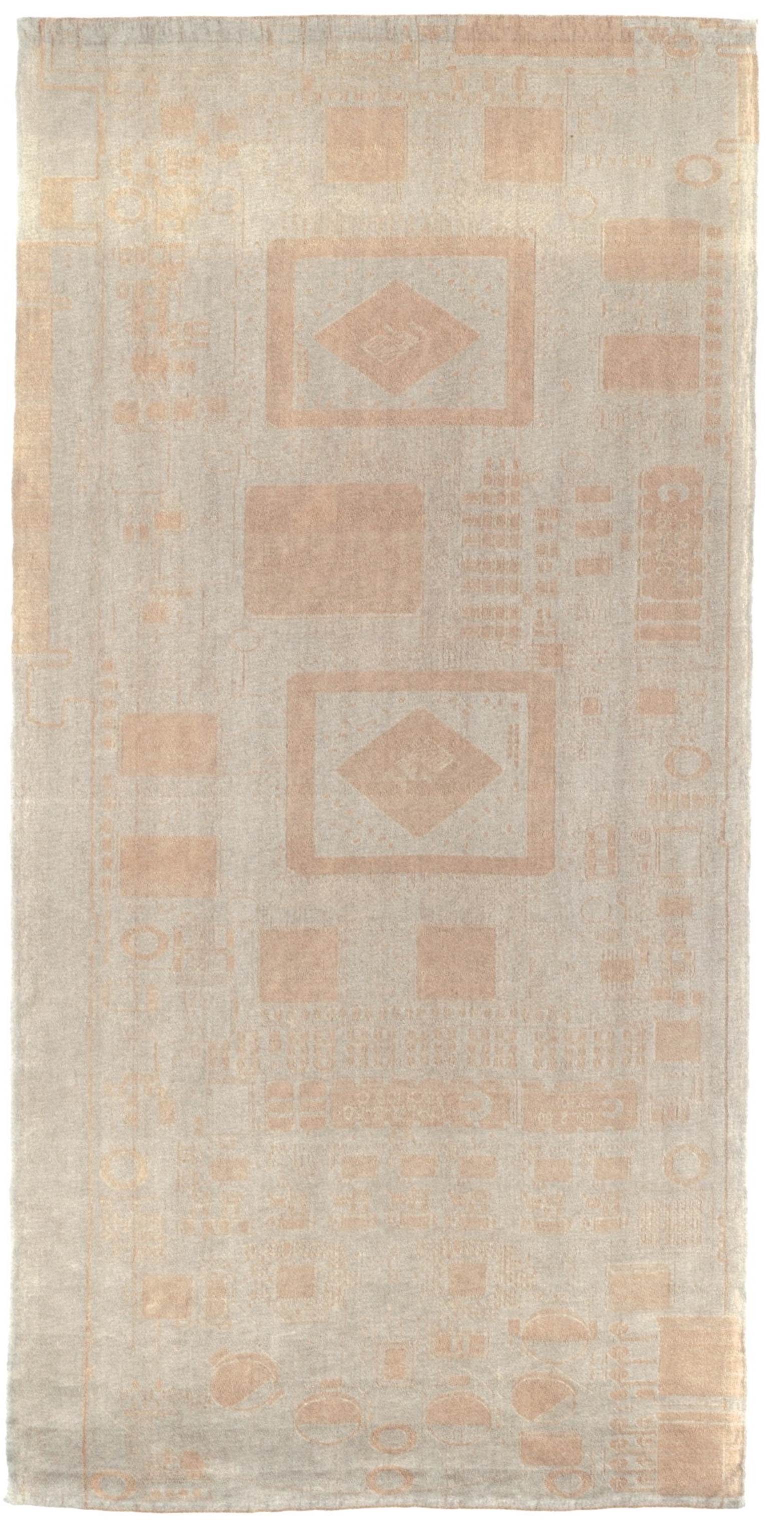

Plate 27

Analia Saban (Argentine, born 1980)
Copper Tapestry (ATI Radeon HD 5970 Graphics Card, AMD, 2009). 2020
Woven copper wire and linen thread
138 ½ × 71 ¼" (351.8 × 181 cm)

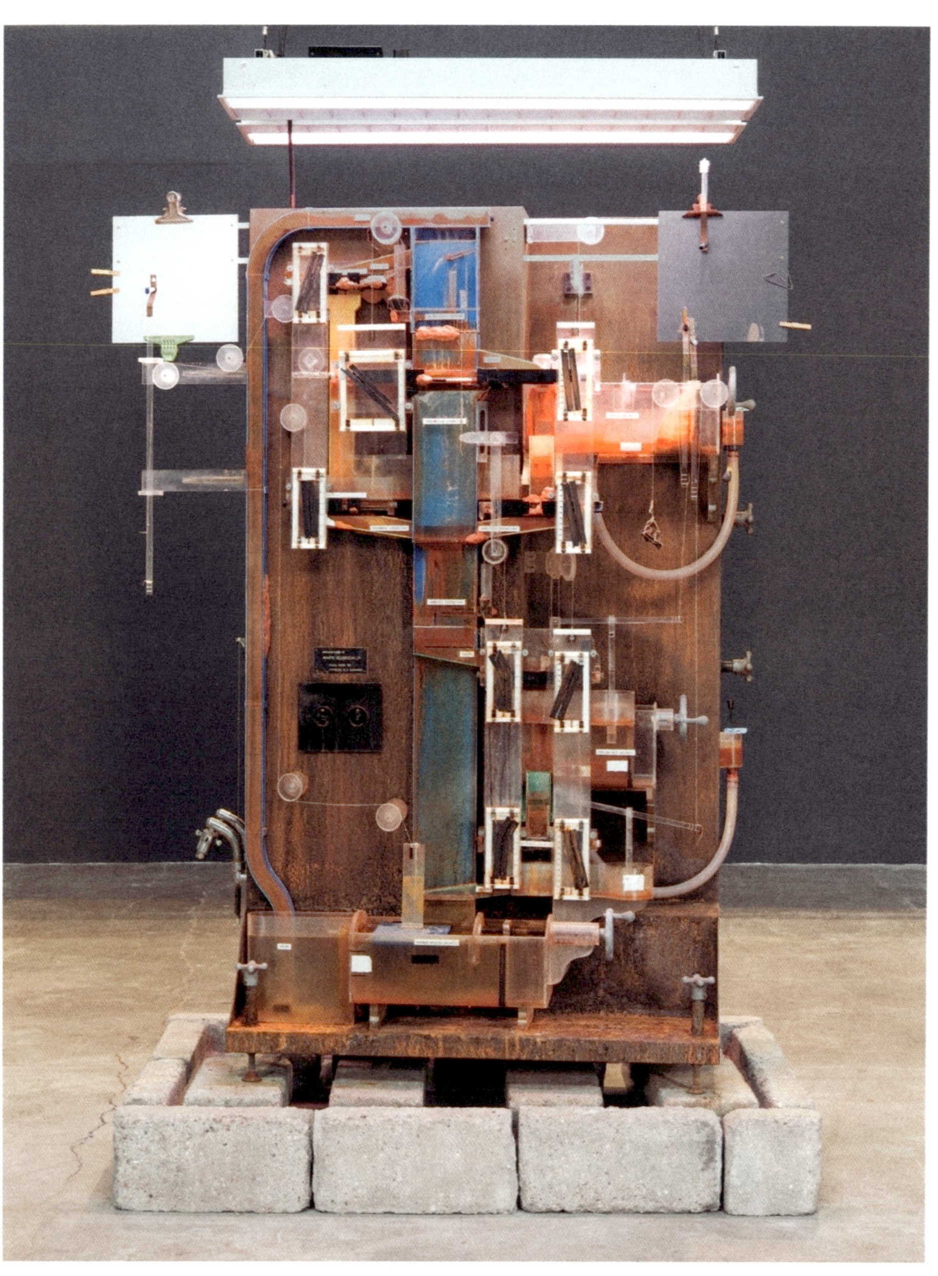

Plate 28

Michael Stevenson (New Zealander, born 1964)
The Fountain of Prosperity (Answers to Some Questions about Bananas). 2006
Plexiglass, steel, brass, aluminum, rubber, cork, string, concrete, dyed water, pumps, and fluorescent lamps
96 7/16 × 62 13/16 × 43 11/16" (245 × 157 × 111 cm)

I

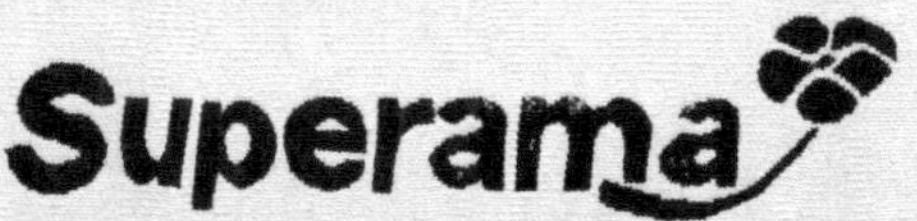

Plate 29

Gabriel Kuri (Mexican, born 1970)
Sin título (Superama II) (*Untitled [Superama II]*). 2005
Wool
44 ½ × 91 ⁵⁄₁₆" (113 × 232 cm)

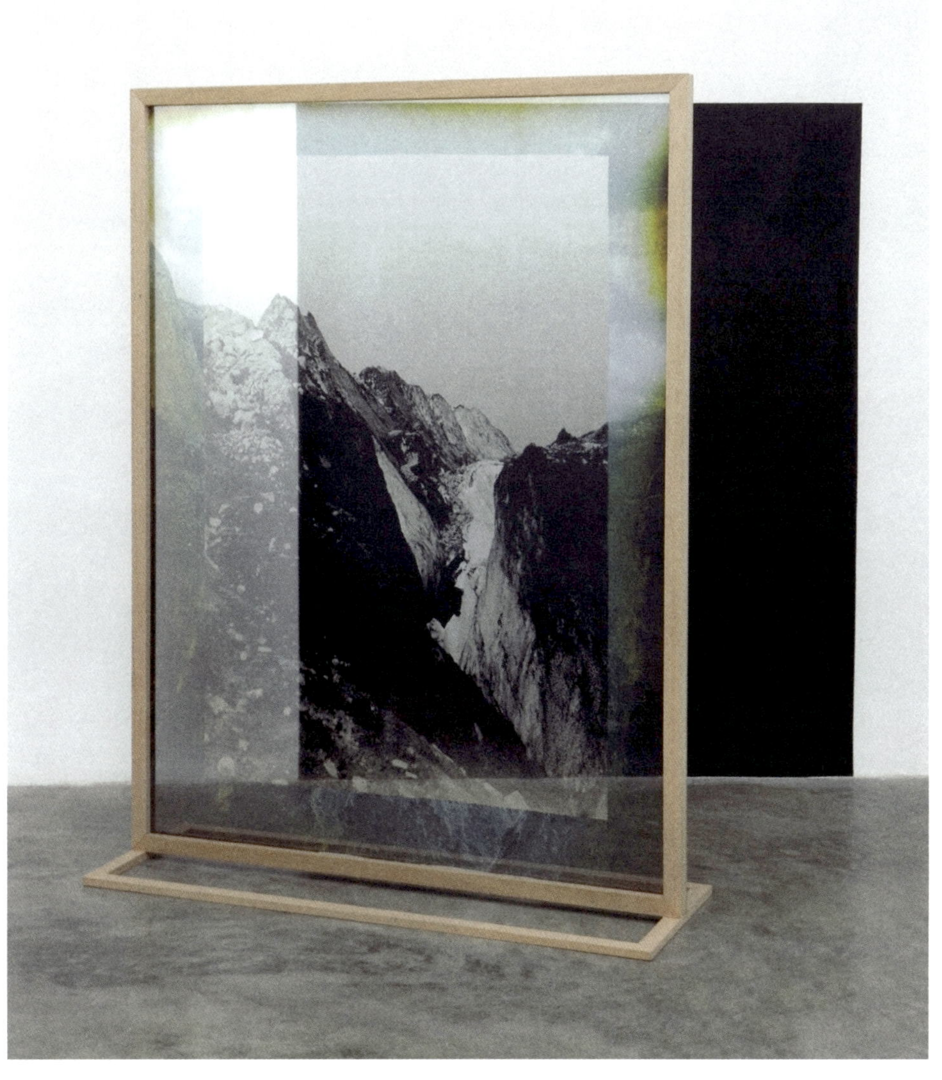

Plate 30

Elena Damiani (Peruvian, born 1979)
Fading Field No. 1. 2012
Inkjet print on silk chiffon with wooden frame and black wall
69 ¾ × 52 ⅞" (177.2 × 134.3 cm)

II

Reverberations

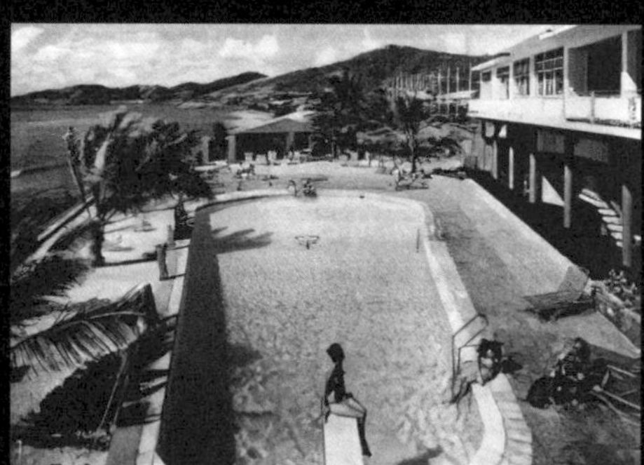

Mario García Torres, *Je ne sais si c'en est la cause.*
2009

II

As mentioned at the beginning of this essay, recent decades have seen a radical re-definition of the field of Latin American art, due to the convergence of several factors: the paradoxical consequences of globalization, the intensification of the ecological crisis, and the impact of decolonial discourse and activism. This section of the exhibition focuses on shifts in the axes of culture toward a reappraisal of artistic languages and movements that, in the boom years of the avant-garde and post-avant-garde, had been forgotten or displaced because they were considered traditionalist, retrograde, minor, or localist. These formal recalibrations correspond to key epistemological, racial, and political changes in the world at large.

Globalization radically changed the configuration, circulation, and, in different phases, the language of Latin American art. By the late 1990s, so-called neo-conceptualism had become the lingua franca of the newly globalized art world. With its emphasis on the narrative capabilities of video and photography, this language was crucial for the translation of local histories in an international arena of ever-increasing interaction and exchange. Neo-conceptualism's distinct emphasis on research is also of particular interest here, since a focus on examining micro and macro histories characterizes the work of many of the artists in this exhibition, especially those of earlier generations such as Katz and Restrepo. These methodologies would produce an explosion of sorts in the late 1990s and early 2000s and are still very relevant today.[28] However, a shift in the dominant languages of contemporary Latin American art that began in the last few decades has also led to the striking emergence of new sensibilities and techniques not previously associated with the contemporary or with global regimes; these include post-Surrealism, vernacular art, and neo-Indigenism.

Another important factor in the redefinition of Latin American art has been the ecological crisis of the Anthropocene and the unexpected transformations it has brought in how artists and intellectuals view their relationships with nature and time—especially in regions that have been severely affected by the environmental deterioration caused by various forms of extractivism. In the immediacy of an unstable, inequitable present and an entropic or perhaps even catastrophic future, modern narratives of progress and development have simply fallen apart, and the cracks and fissures have begun to be filled with other ideas and sensibilities oriented toward nonlinear concepts of time.

This recalibration of how we think about time converges with (and is stimulated by) the emergence of decolonial thought. It was in the 1960s and 1970s that a path toward the de-Westernization of consciousness began to emerge in the work of Latin American artists like Lygia Clark, Hélio Oiticica, and Juan Downey, to name three of the most notable examples. But a new wave of decolonial thinking would sweep through the region in 1992, as a result of debates sparked by celebrations of the five-hundredth anniversary of the "discovery of the Americas"; the rise, all over the continent, of powerful grassroots Indigenous movements, with their cultural and territorial claims; and the advent of popular initiatives that sought to defy the neoliberal shift throughout the 1990s.[29]

28   This focus on investigative practices was particularly clear in Europe, amid a wave of new doctoral programs for artists, along with accompanying networks of institutional and financial support for research projects. Although Latin America did not witness a similar growth of this institutionally sanctioned genre, investigative practices did reach their apex there between the 1990s and the 2010s, as many artists became interested in taking a second look at history.

29   Two critical events along this timeline are the acknowledgment of plurinationality in Ecuador in 1993 and, one year later, the uprising of the Zapatista National Liberation Army in Mexico. Asserting decolonial, ecological, and feminist principles, the Indigenous movement that began in the mountains of Chiapas continues to this day as an autonomy-seeking project. The massive popular uprisings against neoliberal adjustments occurred in Venezuela in 1989 (in the event known as "el Caracazo"), in Mexico in 1994 (prompted by the repression of the Chiapas uprising), in Bolivia between 2000 and 2003 (from the Water War to the Gas War), in Argentina in 2001, and in Chile in 2006 and 2019.

Although in Latin America the theoretical field of decolonial thought has been fraught with intense internal disputes over political legitimacy, in general terms it seeks to dismantle the philosophical tradition imposed by Europeans on the Americas. Based on a dualist worldview (tradition/modernity, magical/scientific thinking, primitivism/civilization, and so on), this outlook, in the words of Peruvian intellectual Aníbal Quijano, positioned Europe as "the exclusive producer and protagonist of modernity."[30] In opposition to this Western cultural monopoly, decolonial thought proposes what theorist Walter Mignolo has defined as a process of "delinking from the colonial matrix of power," through practice, theory, and activism, to create a world of plural epistemologies.[31] In art, this debate facilitated a rethinking of issues essential to our discussion: how to conceive of the past, what to study from the past, and how to gain access to it.

The convergence of these cultural and political processes allows us to understand the current valorization of artistic genealogies that were dismissed by modernity, and the criticism leveled at homogenizing patterns of Western and global art, both fundamental to the works in the second section of the exhibition. One of the most remarkable effects of these developments has been the study, recognition, and reevaluation of Indigenous and Black art as manifestations of survival, relationality, activism, and cultural belonging that are present, fertile—even exemplary. Several works express these axiological twists particularly well: *FOODTOPIA: Después de todo territorio* (*FOODTOPIA: After Every Territory*, 2020), a video by Las Nietas de Nonó; a series of drawings by Sheroanawë Hakihiiwë (2018–21), exhibited in dialogue with photographs by Laura Anderson Barbata (1996–98); and *Mamá Kalunga* (1992) by José Bedia.

Las Nietas de Nonó—siblings mulowayi iyaye nonó and mapenzi chibale nonó—practice a kind of performative art, influenced by experimental theater, through which they explore traumatic episodes of Puerto Rico's Afro-descendant communities. They also have engaged in various forms of community and educational outreach from their family home in the San Antón neighborhood of San Juan, where they live and work.[32] *FOODTOPIA* (plates 32–34) documents an action carried out by Las Nietas during the COVID-19 pandemic. The project consisted of their subsisting, for an extended period, exclusively on food they found through hunting and gathering in the hybrid environment of San Antón—part natural, part industrial. The artists describe their activities during this process as both feminist and decolonial, and the video focuses on their bodies and clothing, as well as their ability to survive as an ancestral skill passed down through the long history of Afro-descendant peoples in the Caribbean.

Instead of excavating formal archives, these artists, like many others in their generation, activate a creativity they associate with the traditionally female task of caring for others. The kind of knowledge they address consists not of forms or techniques (the video documents a collaborative process in which "not knowing" and "doing for the first time" seem essential), but rather a predisposition toward imagination, learning, and adventure as paths toward generating an alternative future. The artists' "foodtopia" finds its starting point in a dystopian present—in which the pandemic has brought on feelings of emptiness and fear of a permanently changed world—and fixes its gaze on a future of ecological sustenance through foraging, the result of recovering a feminism practiced generation after generation in the artists' family. The ancestral element here is a matrix of force, transgression, and survival.

30   Aníbal Quijano, "Coloniality of Power, Eurocentrism, and Latin America," *Nepantla: Views from South* 1, no. 3 (2000): 544.

31   Aïcha Diallo, "A Conversation with Walter Mignolo," *Contemporary And*, August 7, 2014, https://contemporaryand.com/magazines/decolonial-aestheticsaesthesis-has-become-a-connector-across-the-continent/.

32   Inés Katzenstein, "Las Nietas de Nonó: Day-to-Day Utopias," *MoMA Magazine*, April 1, 2022, https://www.moma.org/magazine/articles/716.

The work of Yanomami artist Sheroanawë Hakihiiwë is founded on both his technical skills and his synthetic, precise, and philosophical understanding of natural forms in his native region of the Amazon, which are also applied in geometric patterns traditionally used in basketry and ritual body painting. Hakihiiwë, who lives in Pori Pori, at the edge of the Orinoco River, began making art after meeting the Mexican artist Laura Anderson Barbata when she first came to the Amazon in 1992. There she participated in a sharing of knowledge: in exchange for being taught how to build a canoe out of wood, she offered local workshops on how to make paper from natural fibers. Years later, Hakihiiwë became director of a paper workshop himself and, together with his community, created their first book, *Shapono* (2000, fig. 12), which describes the origin story of building a collective house. Along with the book and several of Hakihiiwë's recent drawings, this exhibition includes photographs taken by Anderson Barbata on her earliest visit to the region (plates 45–48). One particularly telling photograph—a "self-portrait"—replaces the image of the artist typically found in such compositions with a half-built wooden canoe, held up by the person who taught Anderson Barbata how to build it.

Fig. 12   Laura Anderson Barbata and Sheroanawë Hakihiiwë, *Shapono* (Platanal, Venezuela: Yanomami Owë Mamotima and Escuela Intercultural Bilingüe Yanomami, 2000). The Museum of Modern Art Library, New York

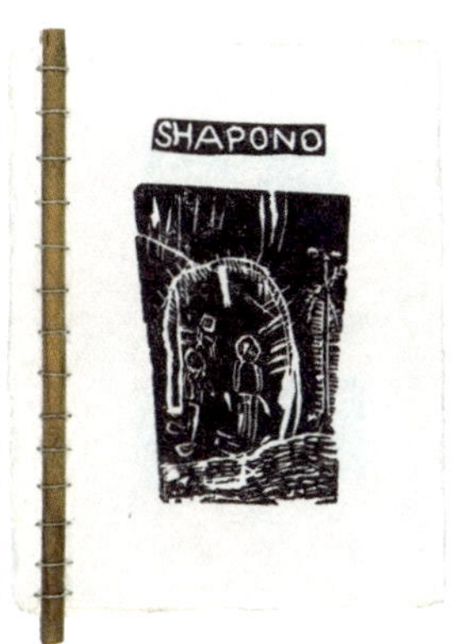

Hakihiiwë's earliest drawings, most of them done on thick, textured handmade paper, were transcriptions and serial repetitions of marks and forms derived from ancestral symbols of his community. More recently, Hakihiiwë began to depict motifs based on direct observation of his environment in the Alto Orinoco: the whiskers of an insect (*Hereremi kaweiki*, 2019) or a shelter fashioned out of palm leaves arranged in a semicircle (*Masiko*, 2018) (plates 42, 43). Hakihiiwë's participation in the contemporary art world is not an anomaly: in the last few years, a number of other Indigenous artists with strong connections to the political and aesthetic legacies of their communities have embraced characteristics and modes of dissemination of the globalized contemporary art system as its aesthetic and political borders have expanded. The challenges that come with the unprecedented visibility of aesthetic traditions that were previously excluded from this system are just beginning to surface.[33]

The opening of the art world to longstanding formal or epistemological repertoires is one result of a movement characterized by what the Portuguese theorist Boaventura de Sousa Santos defines as the "primacy of roots."[34] De Sousa Santos points out the apparent paradox of this intensification of the past emerging precisely at the height of globalization:

> We live in a time of localism and reterritorialization of identities
> and singularities, genealogies and memories. These have become
> all the more visible with the struggles of indigenous people and
> of Afro-descendants in defense of their territories, of peasants in
> defense of their land and against landgrabbing, of tribal peoples
> against megaprojects, and of movements for the right to memory
> after the atrocities of apartheid and dictatorship or movements for
> cultural identity and the right to speak one's own language. In sum,
> the time we live in is also a time of limitless multiplication of roots.[35]

33   This is not the place to discuss the issue in depth, but to synthesize a complex discussion, the situation expands the limits of the concept of contemporary art while also raising important questions about the imbalance of power and the displacement of meaning implied in negotiations with Western aesthetics and institutional frameworks.

34   Boaventura de Sousa Santos, *Epistemologies of the South: Justice Against Epistemicide* (New York: Routledge, 2014), 84.

35   Further on, de Sousa Santos discusses the usefulness of categories like "roots" versus "options," both generated by a logocentric matrix subjecting those concepts to a "criterion of authenticity" that simply is not what it purports to be. *Epistemologies of the South*, 84.

This "multiplication of roots" can be seen in Andrade Tudela's *Huaco deforme* (*Deformed Pottery*) (2012, plates 51–53), a silent film loop that features an ancient urn from the Chancay culture. Due to an irregularity in the firing process, the object was born "deformed," with asymmetrical and uneven contours. The film offers an obsessive close-up of a decorative band that circles the middle of the urn but remains indecipherable for nonexpert viewers. Poised on a pedestal that rotates like a pottery wheel, the urn is presented as if it were an archaeological gem. If Andean cultures have been consistently excluded from the region's more heroic narratives of modernity, Andrade Tudela has turned his attention to an even less valued category of "failed" pieces. In fact, the urn is part of the collection of the Amano Pre-Columbian Textile Museum in Lima, Peru, founded by Yoshitaro Amano (fig. 13). The institution includes "imperfect" bowls, among other pieces, as a way of pointing out what has been excluded from the official canon of pre-Columbian cultures. As the artist explains:

Fig. 13   Yoshitaro Amano collecting ceramics in the Chancay region of Peru, 1975. Archivo Fundación Museo Amano

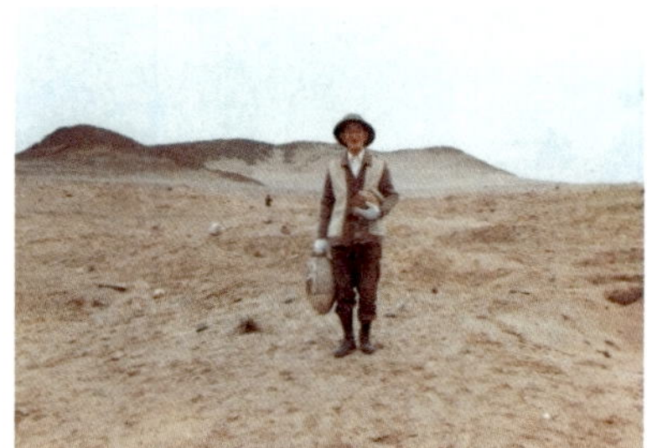

> [My idea] was to rethink [the canon] through the deformed, the unique—like someone looking for a counter-archaeological or counter-modern territory, a negative or autonomous space with regard to our collective heritage. My work swings on a pendulum of sorts, between the personal certainty of belonging to a brutal historical legacy and the need to refute this legacy through my work, with all the tools I have available to me—from the political to the vernacular. . . . *Huaco deforme* is, for me, a way of expressing or manifesting this pendular movement.[36]

The exploration of undervalued or forgotten cultural heritage has very relevant precedents in works by earlier generations of artists, but within quite a different context. Since the beginning of his career in the 1980s, the Cuban José Bedia has informed his painting and drawing practices with a vast knowledge of the myths, languages, and histories of Indigenous and Afro-Cuban cultures, whose art he also avidly collects. *Mamá Kalunga* (1992, plate 50) consists of a semicircular piece of fabric whose very form defies the orthogonal parameters characteristic of Western painting. Its shape comes from the image that it represents: a kind of underworld into which a tiny wooden boat, affixed to the top of the fabric, seems to be sinking. The boat is flanked by two sirens (who may be supporting it or pushing it into the depths) and surrounded by the reverberating waves of a muddy sea that defines the overall composition. In the lower part of the work we find a painted skull crowned with the words "Mamá Kalunga," an allusion to the Bantu deity of fertility and the sea, patron saint of the port of Havana, and Our Lady of Regla.

Two decades later, myth and history would converge again, under new circumstances, in a work by Daniel Steegmann Mangrané titled simply ^ (2013, plate 54). This golden triangle, painted on a wall and illuminated by a spotlight that gives it precise definition, seems to emanate light, referencing the legend of El Dorado, the regenerative power of the sun, and magic. Searching for the "most mystic form possible,"[37] Steegmann Mangrané conceived the work for the 2012 exhibition *Alphabet of the Magi*, which sought to present different "codification(s) of transcendentalism."[38] At the time, he said, "What interests me is creating things that invite the imagination but, in some way, leave you feeling uncertain because

36   Interview with Armando Andrade Tudela by Madeline Murphy Turner, April–November 2020, "Study of the Cisneros Gift."

37   Daniel Steegmann Mangrané, telephone conversation with the author, June 2022.

38   Press release for the exhibition *Alphabet of the Magi*, Mendes Wood DM, São Paulo, 2012.

you aren't sure what they mean." The title, for instance, "is an unpronounceable circumflex accent that is used in just a few languages and has a somewhat formal connection to the piece."[39] In addition to an affinity with works by Blinky Palermo, Mathias Goeritz, and Luis Barragán, who hover over the piece like formal or spiritual ghosts, there are evident resonances with Indigenous geometries, no doubt linked to the in-depth research Steegmann Mangrané has done on the spatiality, spectrality, and psychedelia of the Indigenous communities of the Amazon.

The notion of roots, in this exhibition, is not always continuous, nor is it always linked to an Oedipal, vertical genealogy by blood. Cultural references can also be elective, in the most expansive traditions of Borgesian anti-nationalism or of Queer kinship beyond the nuclear family (however distant these perspectives may be from each other). Mexican artist Mario García Torres has assiduously pursued an investigation of overlooked chapters in the annals of Western art history (especially Conceptual art), as a way to complicate notions of fiction and storytelling, and to research and create a speculative genealogy for himself. As documented in his work *Je ne sais si c'en est la cause* (2009, plates 39–41), he embarks on a quest to find a group of murals that Daniel Buren created over the course of two separate visits to a hotel on the Caribbean island of Saint Croix in the early 1960s.[40] García Torres's goal was not only to unearth what were said to be the French artist's first site-specific works, prefiguring his characteristic vertical stripe compositions; he also wanted to test Buren's own statement about the Mexican muralists' influence on his early work, particularly in relation to his rejection of conventional formats of painting.

Once he arrived in Saint Croix, however, García Torres's focus shifted, and his narrative came to incorporate the dramatic story of the Grapetree Bay Hotel, the site of the murals and a symbol of the failed promises of development in the Caribbean. The artist found himself in a place that, like many others, had suffered a precipitous decline in tourism, caused, in part, by the negative reputation the island acquired after a shooting at a local golf club in 1972. Hurricane Hugo, which brought massive devastation to the area in 1989, added to the severity of these lean years. The general state of ruin that the artist found at the hotel therefore informed his narrative, which combines historical documentation, music, and images, describing a lost chapter of European art intertwined with the history of tourism as an industry of extraction in the Caribbean (fig. 14).[41]

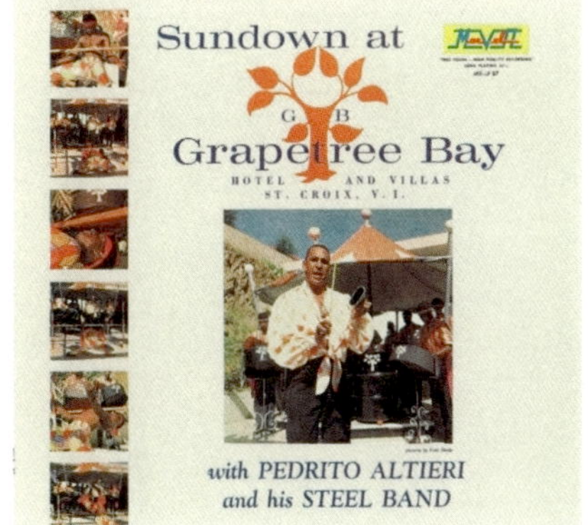

Fig. 14   *Sundown at Grapetree Bay with Pedrito Altieri and his Steel Band*, 1962. Vinyl LP from a collection of memorabilia gathered by Mario García Torres as part of *Je ne sais si c'en est la cause* (2009)

39   *Alphabet of the Magi* press release.

40   For more information on these early pieces that Buren painted in the Virgin Islands and their "virginizing" function, according to Buren's ironic way of thinking, see Alison Gingeras, *The Eye of the Storm: Works in Situ by Daniel Buren* (New York: Solomon R. Guggenheim Museum, 2005).

41   García Torres had already worked on the connections between art history and the tourist industry. See, for example, his 2005 video *Carta Abierta a Doctor Atl* (*Open Letter to Dr. Atl*), in which he talks about the culture industries' predatory relationship with the landscape.

II

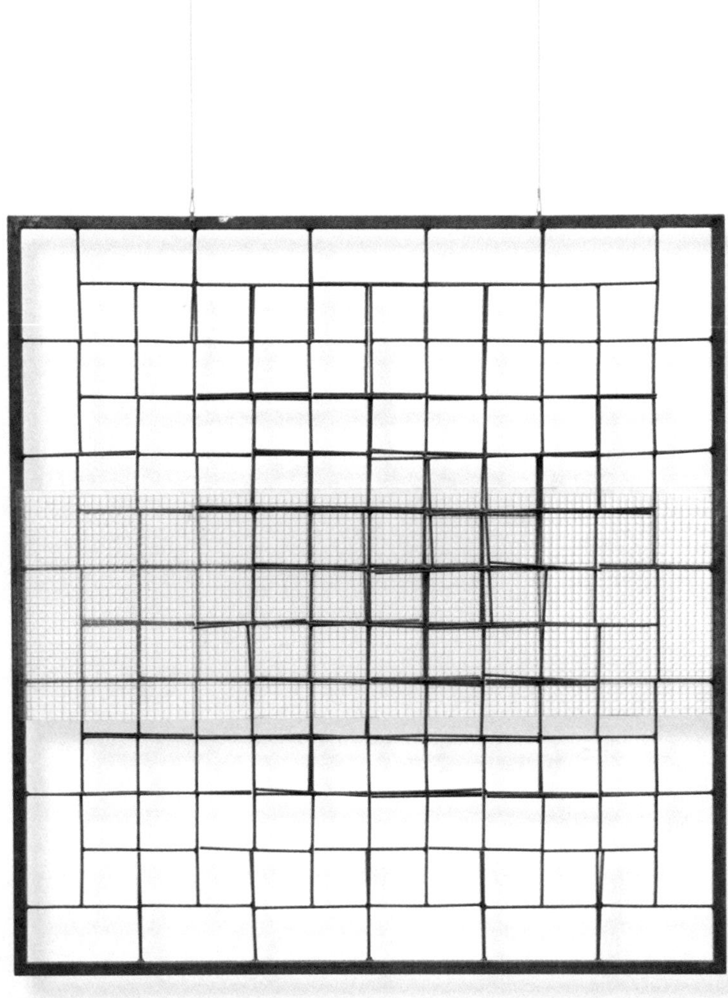

Cildo Meireles (Brazilian, born 1948)
Malhas da liberdade (*Meshes of Freedom*). 1976/1977
Iron and glass
47 ¼ × 48 ¼ × 1 ½" (120 × 122.6 × 3.8 cm)

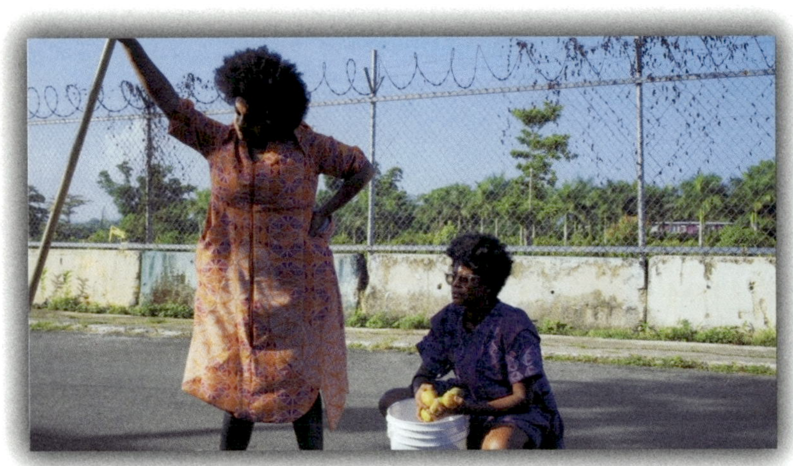

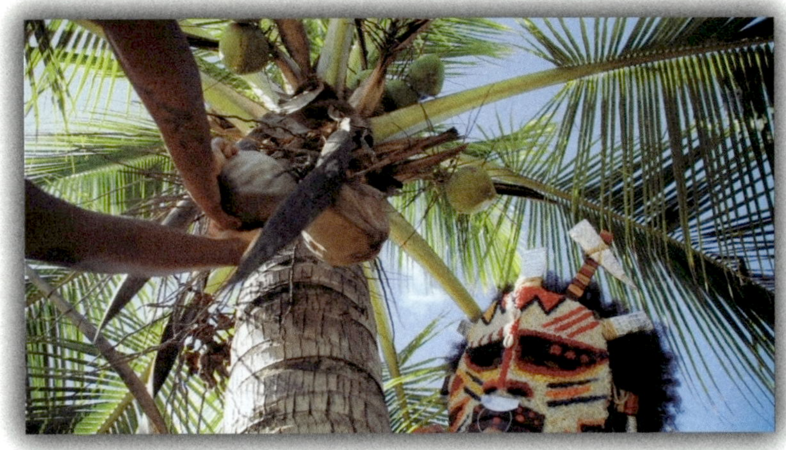

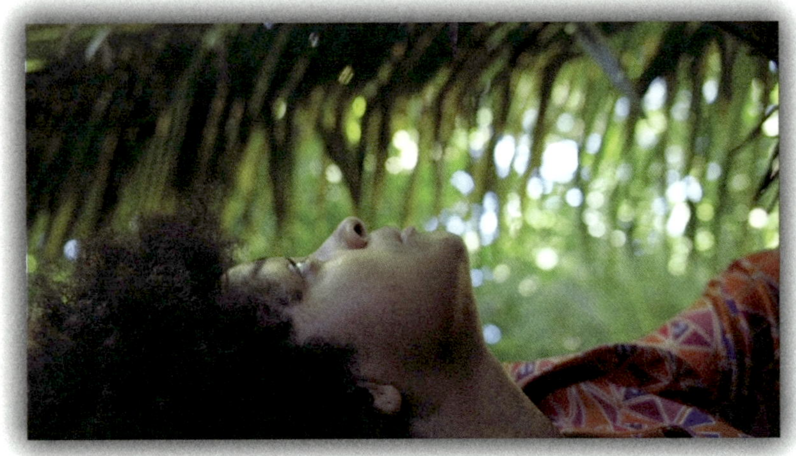

Plates 32–34

Las Nietas de Nonó (Afro-Caribbean, est. 2011)
mulowayi iyaye nonó (Puerto Rican, born 1979) and
mapenzi chibale nonó (Puerto Rican, born 1982)
FOODTOPIA: Después de todo territorio
(*FOODTOPIA: After Every Territory*). 2020
Video (color, sound), 27:54 min.

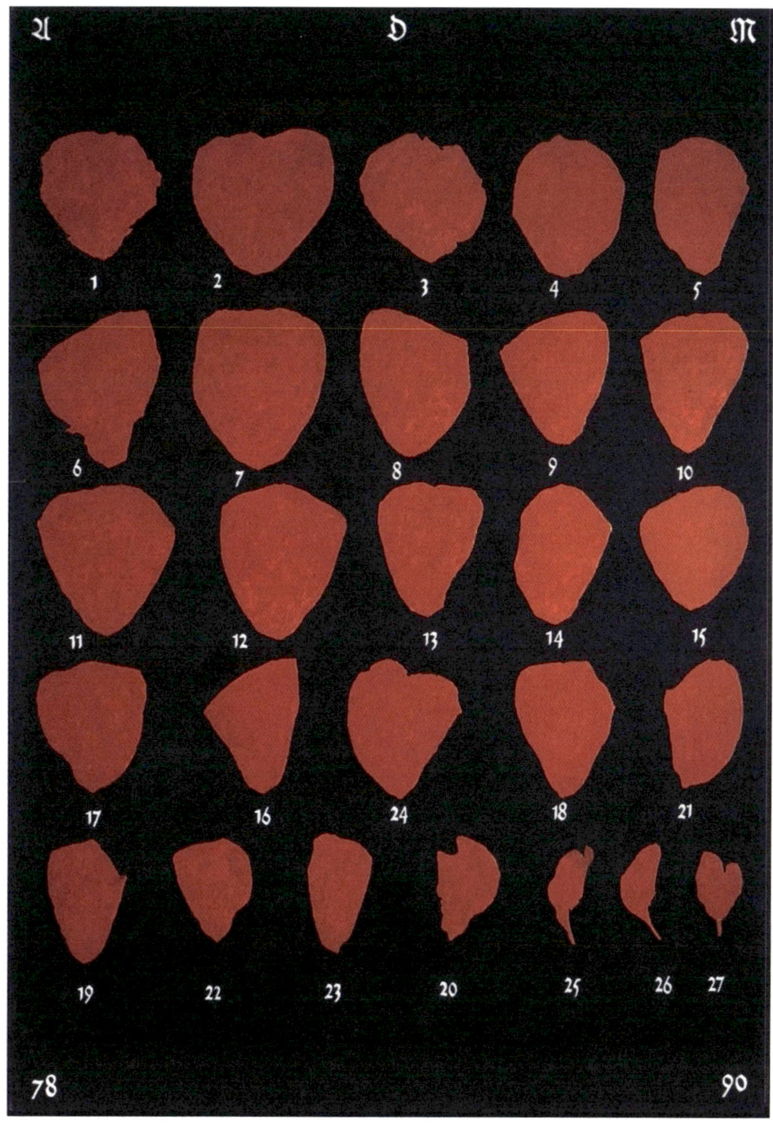

Plate 35

Roberto Obregón (Venezuelan, born Colombia. 1946–2003)
ADM. 1978–90
Acrylic on paper and canvas
52 ¼ × 37 ¼" (132.7 × 94.6 cm)

67

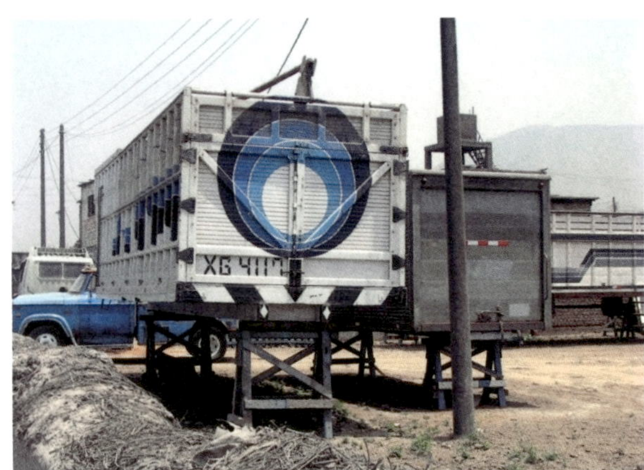

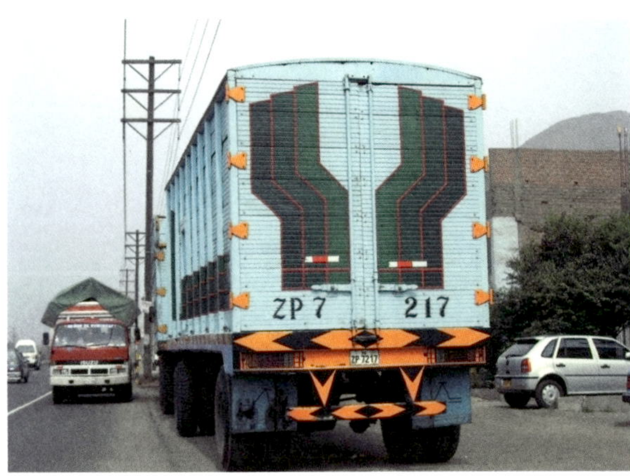

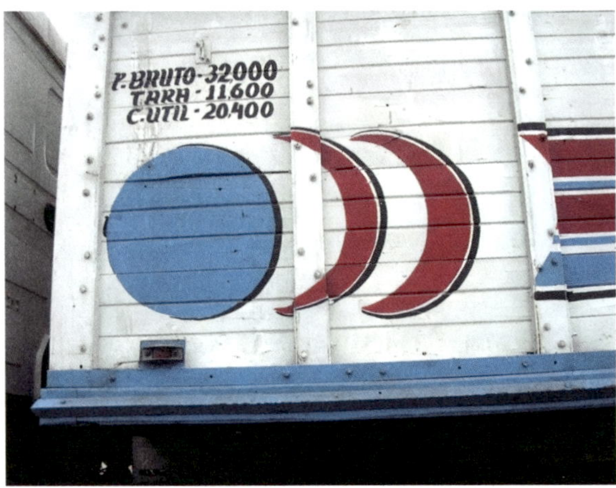

Armando Andrade Tudela (Peruvian, born 1975)
Camión (*Truck*). 2003
Sixty 35mm color slides, 5 min. loop

68

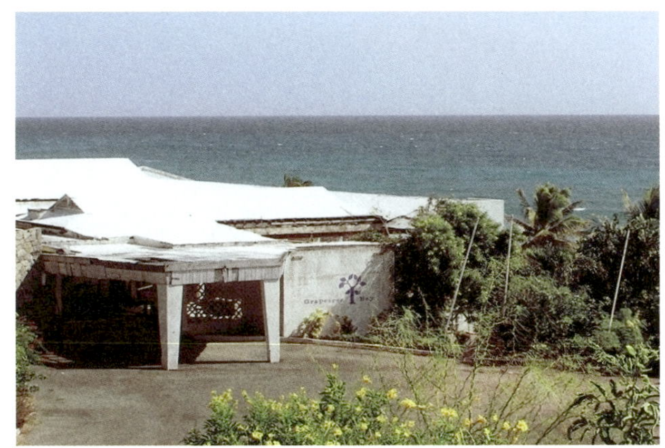

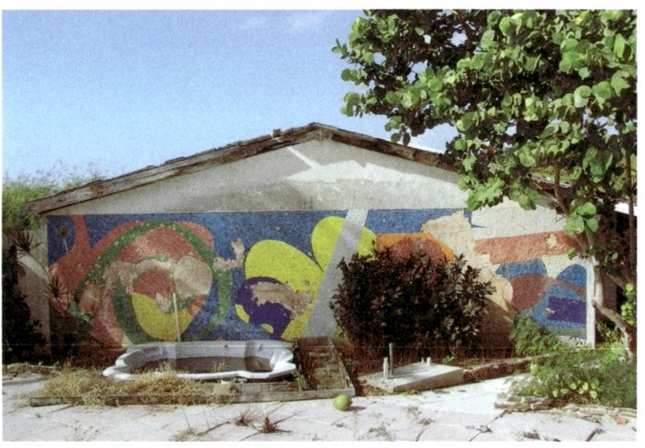

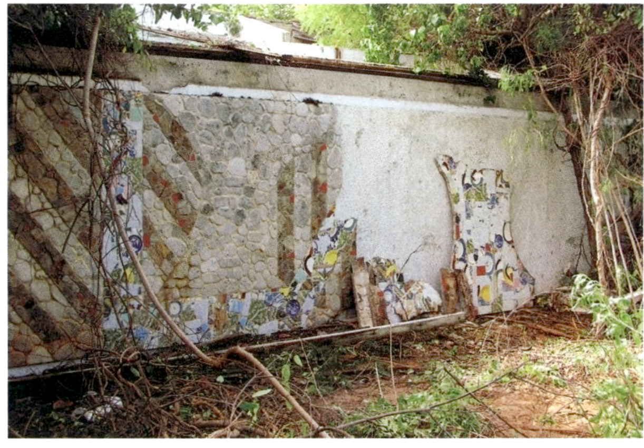

Plates 39–41

Mario García Torres (Mexican, born 1975)
Je ne sais si c'en est la cause. 2009
Fifty-eight 35mm color slides and two vinyl LPs
Dimensions variable

69

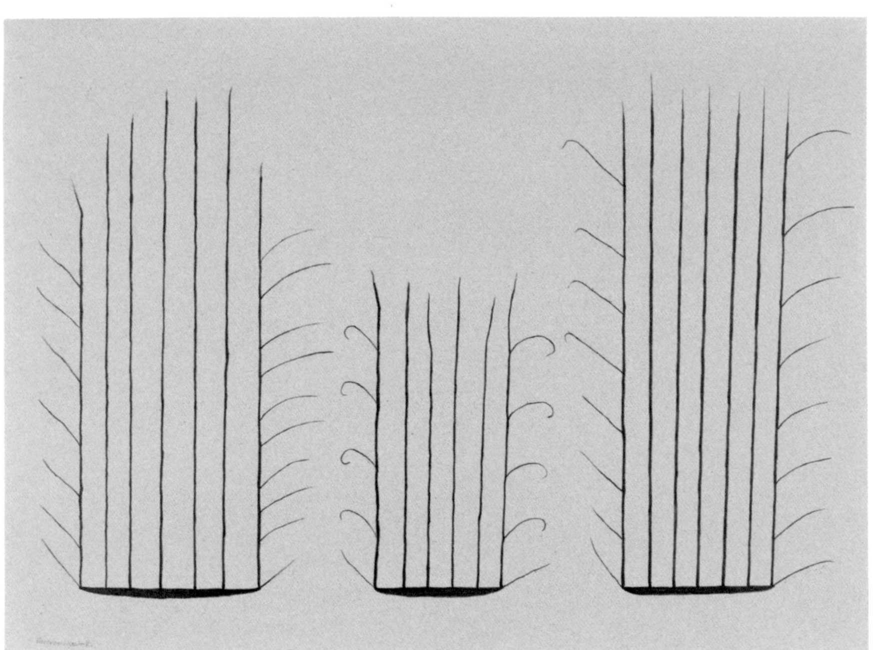

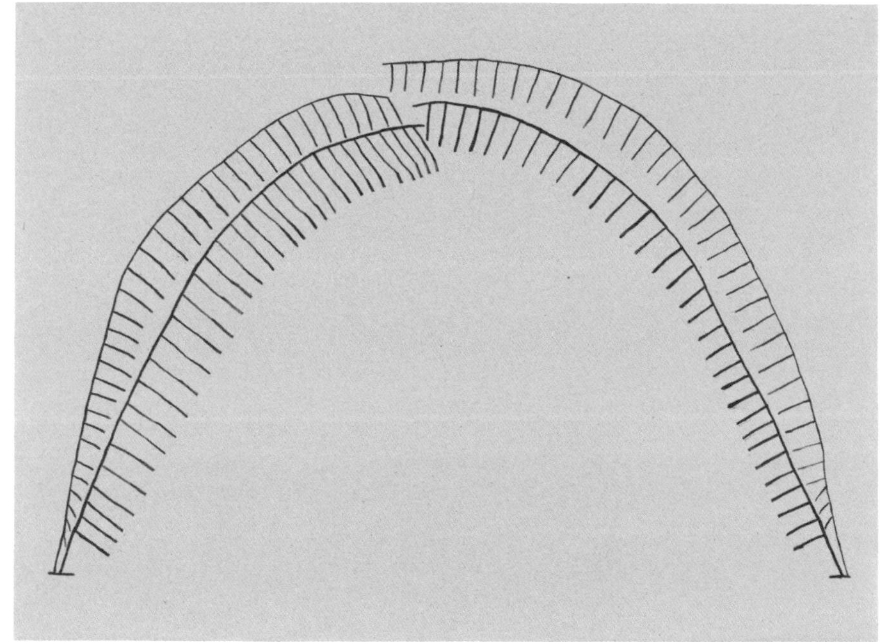

Plate 42

Sheroanawë Hakihiiwë (Venezuelan and Yanomami, born 1971)
Hereremi kaweiki (*Beard of an Insect*). 2019
Ink on paper
19 ¾ × 27 ½" (50.2 × 69.9 cm)

Plate 43

Sheroanawë Hakihiiwë (Venezuelan and Yanomami, born 1971)
Masiko (*Shelter*). 2018
Acrylic on paper
19 ¾ × 27 ⁹⁄₁₆" (50.2 × 70 cm)

70

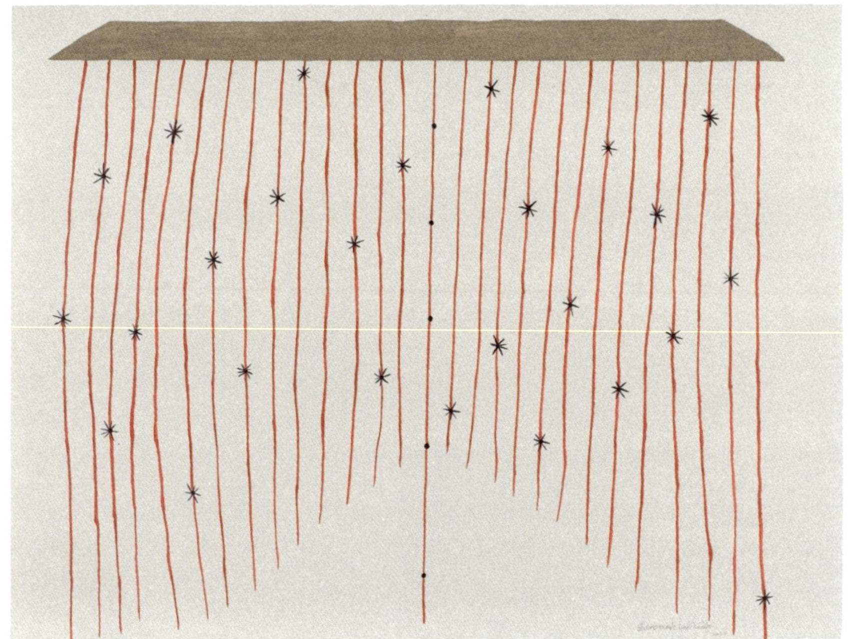

Plate 44

Sheroanawë Hakihiiwë (Venezuelan and Yanomami, born 1971)
Shihitima thothope (*Stinging Vine*). 2020
Acrylic on colored paper
19 ⅞ × 26 ¾" (50.5 × 68 cm)

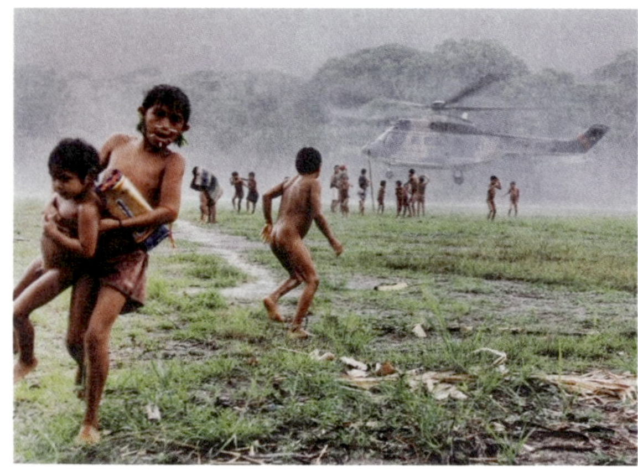
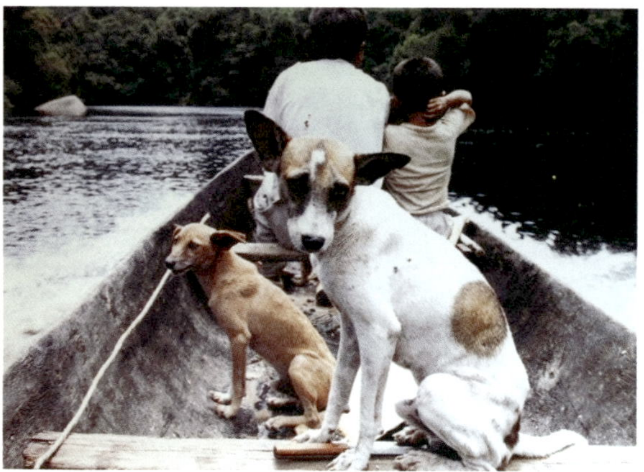
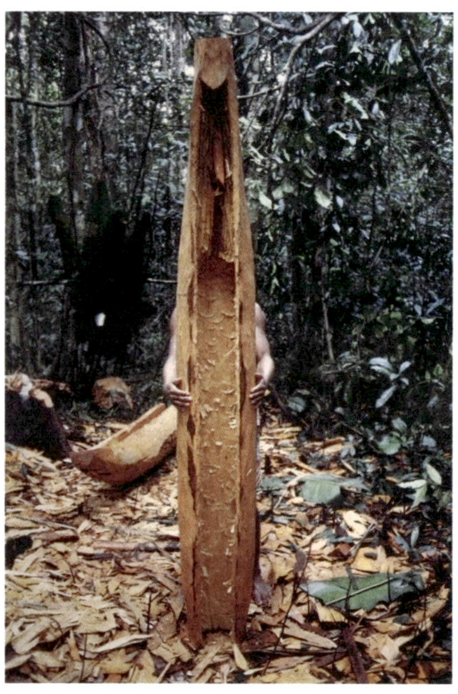
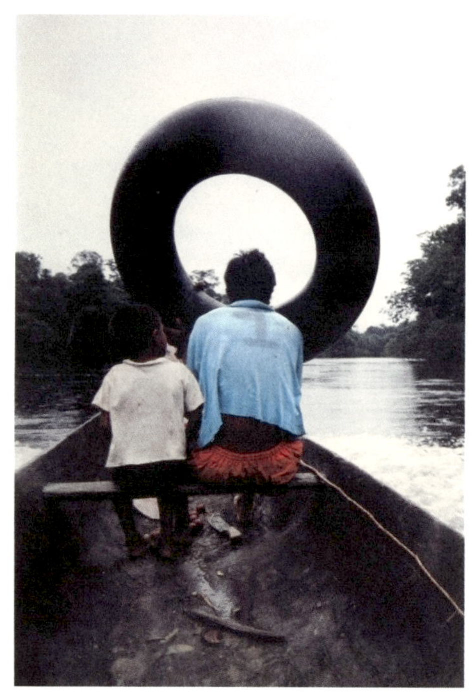

Plate 45

Laura Anderson Barbata (Mexican, born 1958)
En el orden del caos (*In the Order of Chaos*), from Intercambios,
Amazonas Venezuela (Exchanges, Amazonas Venezuela). 1996–98
Silver dye bleach print
13 × 16" (33 × 40.6 cm)
Colección Patricia Phelps de Cisneros

Plate 46

Laura Anderson Barbata (Mexican, born 1958)
Conejo, from Intercambios, Amazonas Venezuela (Exchanges,
Amazonas Venezuela). 1996–98
Silver dye bleach print
13 × 16" (33 × 40.6 cm)
Colección Patricia Phelps de Cisneros

Plate 47

Laura Anderson Barbata (Mexican, born 1958)
Autorretrato (*Self-Portrait*), from Intercambios, Amazonas Venezuela
(Exchanges, Amazonas Venezuela). 1996–98
Silver dye bleach print
16 × 13" (40.6 × 33 cm)
Colección Patricia Phelps de Cisneros

Plate 48

Laura Anderson Barbata (Mexican, born 1958)
Rober, from Intercambios, Amazonas Venezuela (Exchanges,
Amazonas Venezuela). 1996–98
Silver dye bleach print
16 × 13" (40.6 × 33 cm)
Colección Patricia Phelps de Cisneros

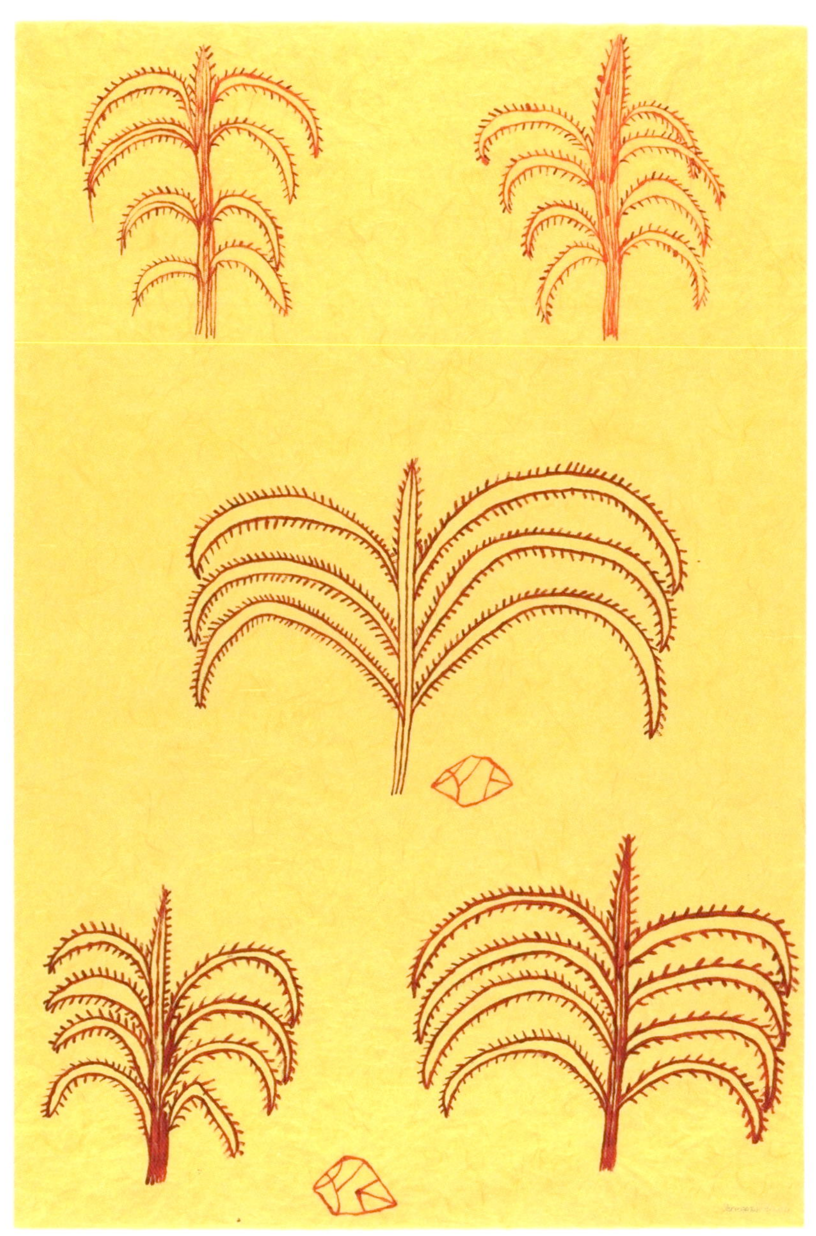

Plate 49

Sheroanawë Hakihiiwë (Venezuelan and Yanomami, born 1971)
Sitio Siki (*Bromeliads*). 2021
Acrylic on colored paper
37 × 25" (94 × 63.5 cm)

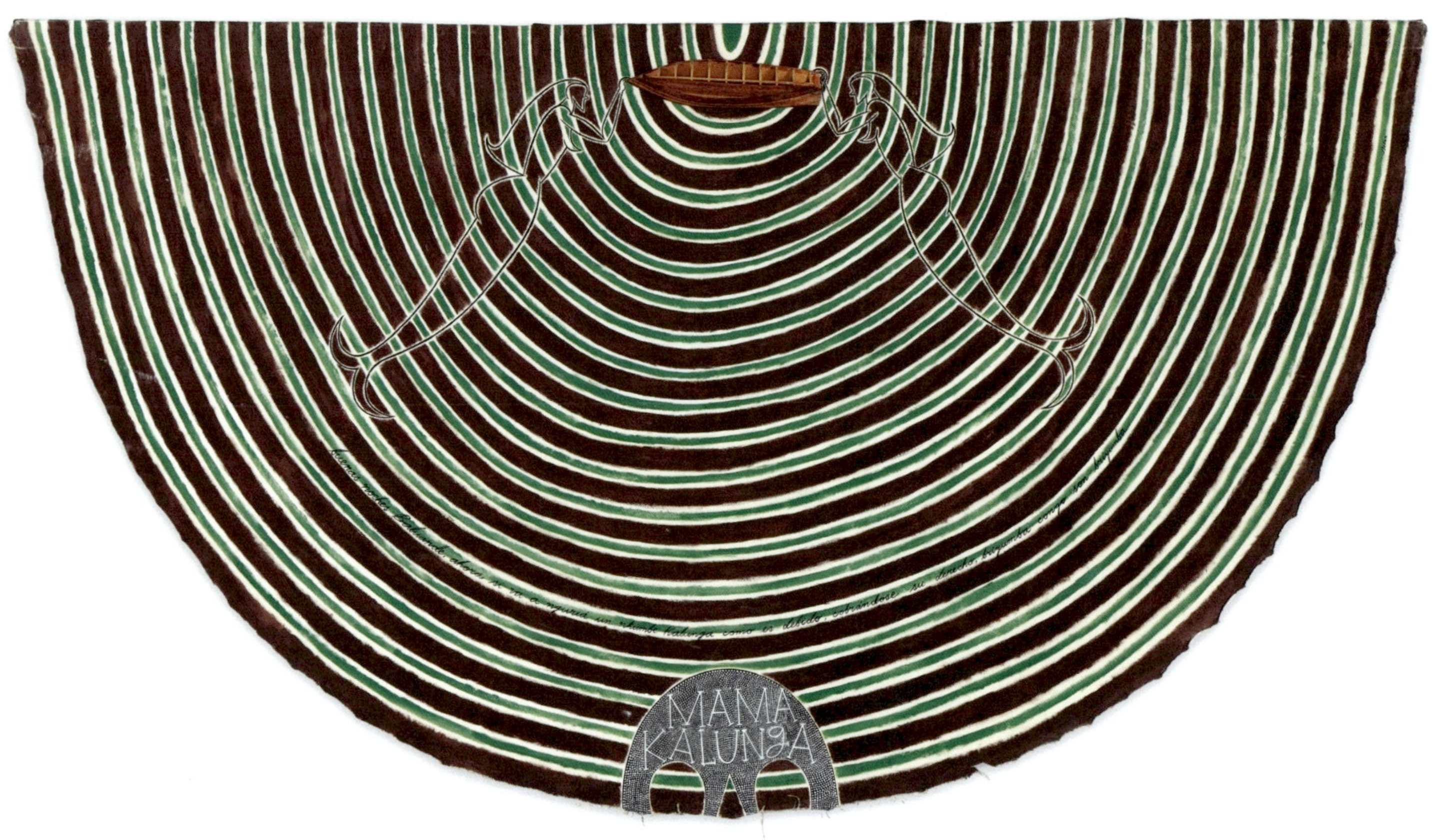

José Bedia (Cuban, born 1959)
Mamá Kalunga. 1992
Acrylic and wood on canvas
66 ¹⁵⁄₁₆ × 118 ⅛ × 4" (170 × 300 × 10.2 cm)
Colección Patricia Phelps de Cisneros

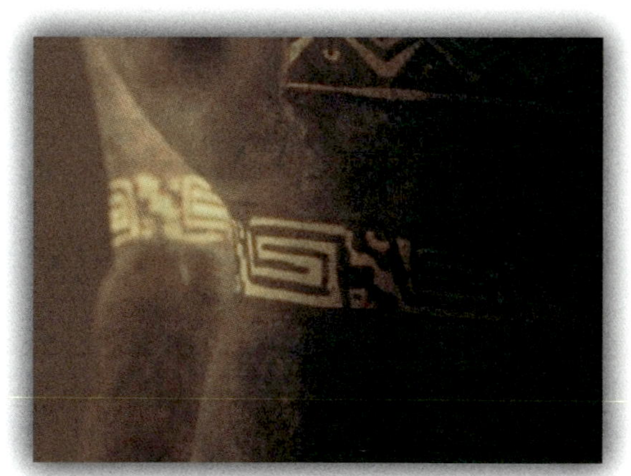

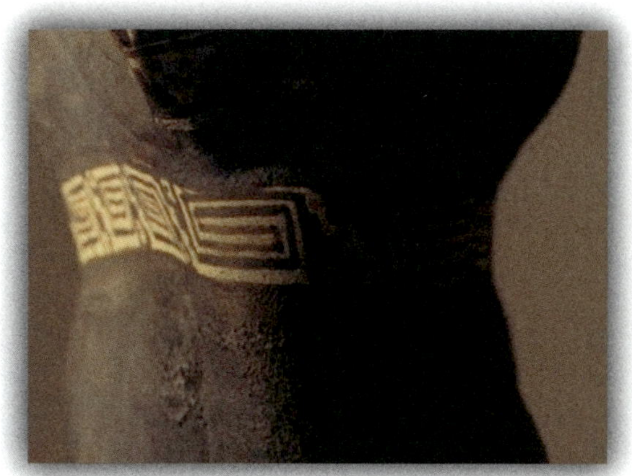

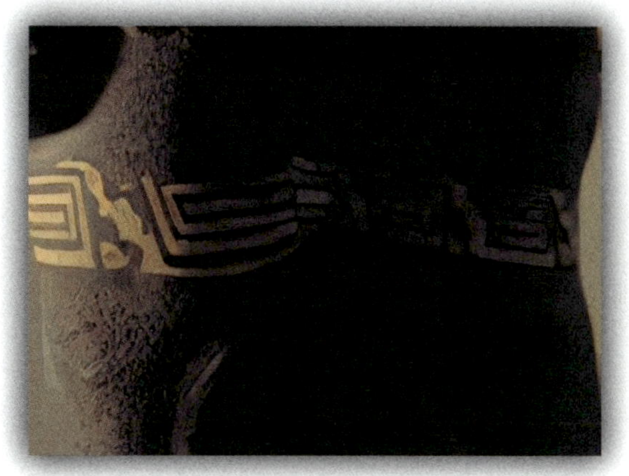

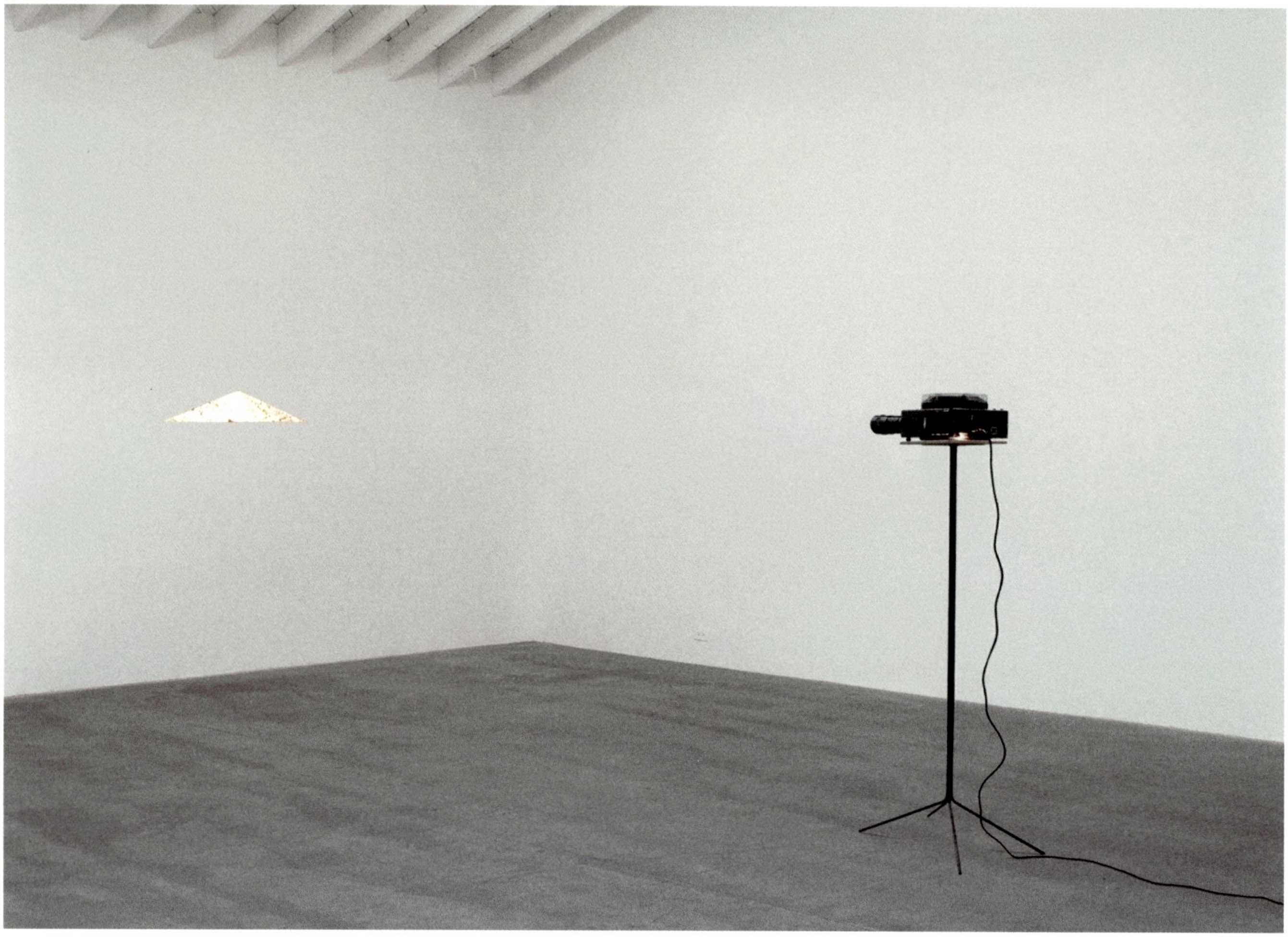

Plate 54

Daniel Steegmann Mangrané (Spanish and Brazilian, born 1977)
^ . 2013
35mm color slide, slide projection equipment, and gold leaf
65 × 36 × 55" (165.1 × 91.4 × 139.7 cm)
Collection of Adriana Cisneros de Griffin

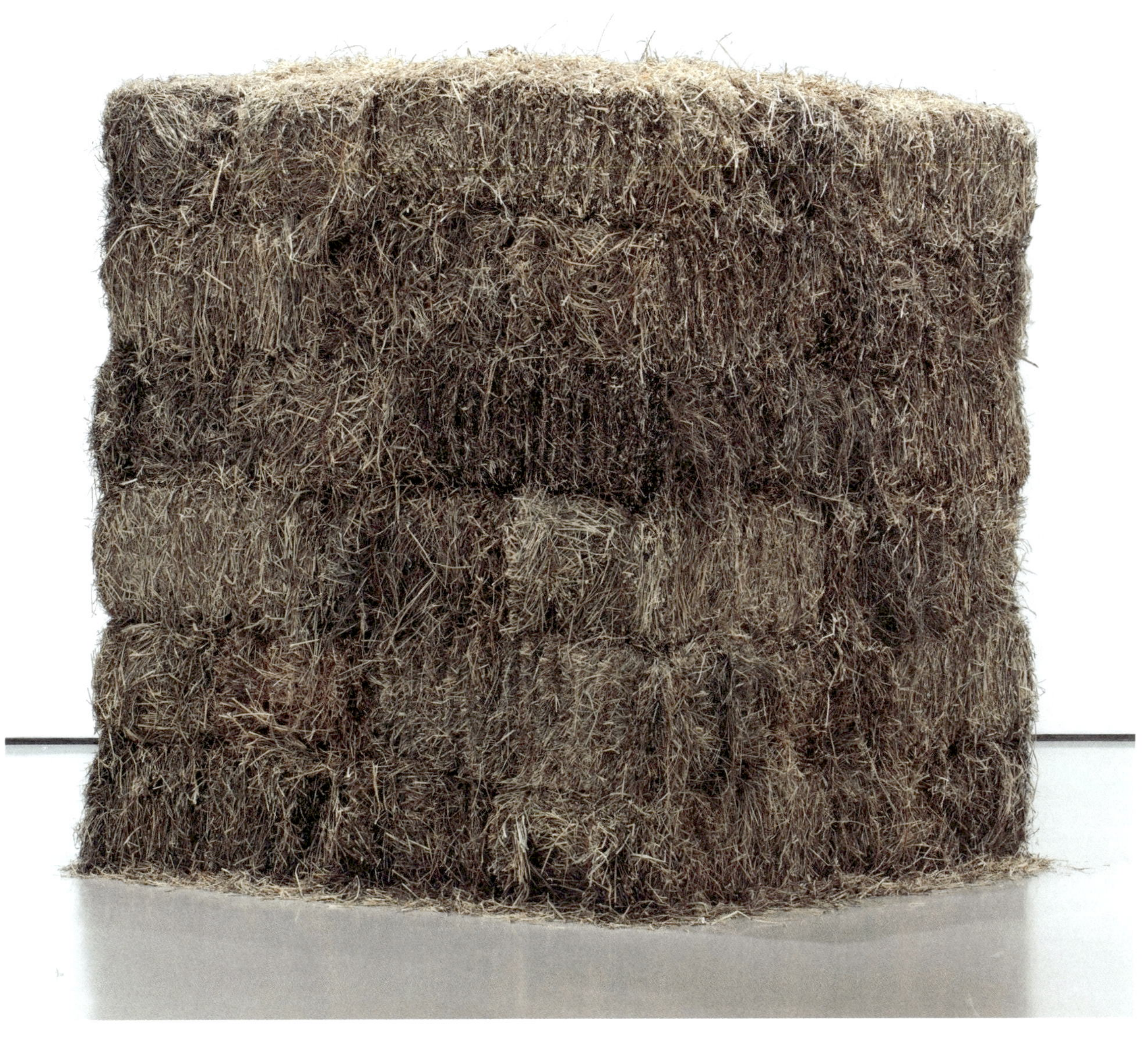

Cildo Meireles (Brazilian, born 1948)
Fio (*Thread*). 1990–95
Forty-eight bales of hay, one 18-carat gold needle, and
100 meters of gold thread
Approximately 85 × 73 × 72" (215.9 × 185.4 × 182.9 cm)

III

Kinships

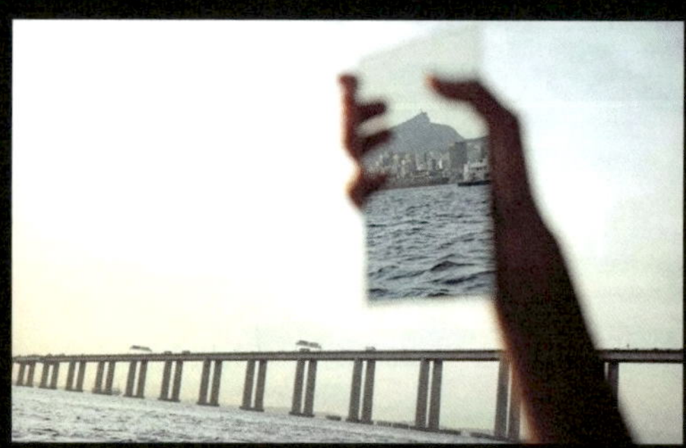

Aline Motta. *(Outros) Fundamentos ([Other] Foundations)*. 2017–19

III

The third and final section of the exhibition proposes a change in perspective. The artists here do not engage with (or critique) the long histories of modernity, or embrace cultural traditions reclaimed through processes of reconstruction or continuity. Instead, they explore the unstable, fragile nature of memory as an essential part of life, and suggest ways that art may function as a powerful mnemonic device, both in the public realm and on a more intimate scale. The focus shifts to affective histories: while some works allude to the evanescence of memory and technologies of remembering, others depict kinship ties as a means of building community and continuity across diverse temporalities. The question of death and the challenge to memory that it poses for the living pervade almost every artwork in this group.

One anchor of the section is the philosophical drama implicit in registering the process of dying as it appears in the film *Present Memory* (2009, plates 61, 62), by Uruguayan artist Alejandro Cesarco. The protagonist of this piece is the artist's father, an elderly man with an old-fashioned moustache, who seems to be ill. Peering into the camera blankly, he sits motionless, as if posing for a still rather than a moving image. The camera captures him in his medical office (a bit antiquated, like the doctor himself) with a melancholy that implies an acknowledgment of this recorded image as a document of final contact, of farewell. The camera lingers on the instantaneous yet static moment of the photographic pose, and as the film advances we begin to realize that what we are seeing is actually the projection of another projection. A *mise en abyme*, the film is projected in the same space in which it was filmed, suggesting that the space has already been transformed into one of absence.

Cesarco has devoted his artistic career to exploring matters of love as seen through the lens offered by film history, literary narratives, and the rhetorical tradition of Conceptual art. His works might be compilations of book dedications, indices of nonexistent books, receipts for transactions, translations, or reproductions of scenes from the annals of film, among other preexisting structures, but they most often index matters of the heart. *Present Memory* lingers on the body of Cesarco's father, only to later plunge into the abyss of time and death. The work is, in the artist's words, "a portrait of my father, shortly after he had been diagnosed with lung cancer." He explains:

> I filmed him in his office . . . using a hand-held 16mm camera and later projected what I had filmed onto the same wall and recorded that projection on video. The work documents both a constructed and an anticipated memory. The literal and metaphorical projection staged in the work is a rehearsal of fears: an attempt at dealing with a future absence, the process of mourning and remembering, mortality and letting go. It was, in a way, an attempt at managing or controlling the feeling of loss by anticipating someone's absence.[42]

The death of a father is also the subject of *Heritage* (2007, plate 1), a video by Brazilian artist Thiago Rocha Pitta. It documents a ritual imagined by his father (an artist as well), in which two trees are thrown onto a boat foundering in the ocean. The ritual, realized by Rocha Pitta after his father's death, ended with the burial of an actual boat on the artist's property in Rio de Janeiro (figs. 15, 16). A more politicized vision of mourning emerges in the 2014 video work *Antropologia do negro II* (*Black Anthropology II*), by Paulo Nazareth, also from Brazil. The relationship to the dead is once again filial, but here it is presented as part of a history of racial violence. Nazareth's best-known work, *Noticias de América* (*News from America*, 2011), consisted of a ten-month journey he made between Belo Horizonte, Brazil, and Florida, mostly on foot. With a spirit somewhere between religious and anthropological, the artist sought to gain knowledge of the continent while undergoing self-inflicted suffering.

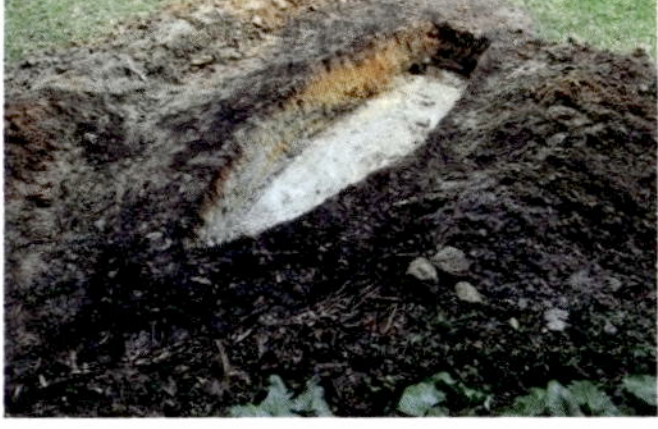

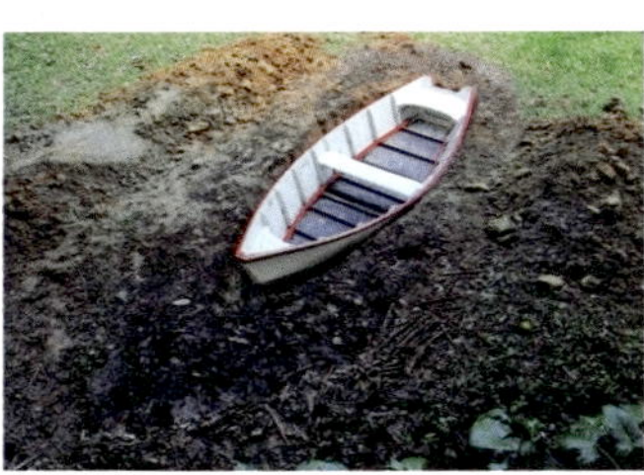

Figs. 15, 16 Thiago Rocha Pitta. *Inland Shipwreck*. 2008. Inkjet prints, 11 ¹³⁄₁₆ × 15 ¾" (30 × 40 cm)

42   Interview with Alejandro Cesarco by Madeline Murphy Turner, June 15, 2020, "Study of the Cisneros Gift."

Antropologia do negro II (plates 69–71) takes up a bit of that sacrificial quest. In the archives of the Museu Antropológico Estácio de Lima, a museum in Salvador de Bahia, Brazil, that operated from 1958 to 2005, Nazareth found a collection of human skulls assembled in the name of positivist science and criminal anthropology. Enacting a ritual, he lies on the floor and proceeds to cover his head with the skulls, reaching for them one by one. In this makeshift burial mound, the artist has placed himself physically at the level of the bones and summoned a kind of phantasmic dimension. And if mourning is the state produced when the shadow of a lost object invades the subject, then here Nazareth stages an "enshadowing" as a testimony of compassion for the abuses suffered by Black communities in Brazil (figs. 17, 18).

Fig. 17   Paulo Nazareth. *CA – sem titulo [direito ao funeral] – salvador – bahia – Brasil – 2014 (CA – Untitled [Right to Funeral] – Salvador – Bahia – Brazil – 2014)*, 2014. Offset print on paper

Fig. 18   Paulo Nazareth. Pamphlet for the Bienal da Bahia, 2014. Offset print on paper

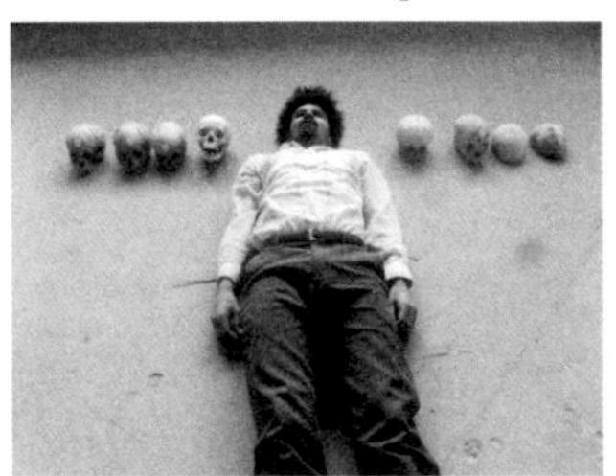

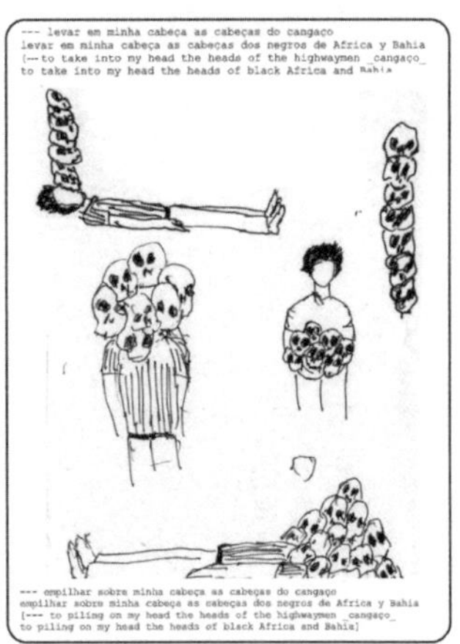

Nazareth's symbolic act of sacrifice is linked to Paul Ricoeur's concept of owing a debt to the dead: "As soon as the idea of a debt to the dead, to people of flesh and blood to whom something really happened in the past, stops giving documentary research its highest end, history loses its meaning."[43] Nazareth understands that perspective on history. Moreover, by alluding to a debt to the past, his work cannot help but recall Saidiya Hartman's essential question: "Can beauty provide an antidote to dishonor, and love a way to 'exhume buried cries' and reanimate the dead?"[44] *(Outros) Fundamentos ([Other] Foundations)* (2017–19, plates 57–59), by another Brazilian, Aline Motta, came out of a comparable desire to heal racial wounds through speculative links between Brazil and Africa. Referring to her own family's heritage, the artist says: "We might be fragmented, but we are not broken."[45] In Motta's video, bodies of water in Lagos, Nigeria; Cachoeira, in Salvador de Bahia; and Rio de Janeiro reflect each other in language—their names mean "lakes," "waterfall," and "river"—and in mirrors that search for an analogous place or referent across the horizon.

Mnemonic and affective ties between generations are symbolized as a material, visceral connection in *Por um fio (By a Thread)* (1976/2017, plate 60), a work by the Brazilian artist Anna Maria Maiolino.[46] The photograph features the artist, her mother, and her daughter sitting in a row, connected by a white thread coming out of the older woman's mouth, passing through the artist's mouth, and entering her daughter's (and vice versa), like Lygia Clark's "anthropophagic drool" or like the body-thread manifestation of a current of genetic and affective transmission. The photo also reveals, quite clearly, the physical similarities between the three women, staging "the truth of lineage" that Roland Barthes sees as one of photography's distinguishing characteristics.[47] "Lineage," writes Barthes, "reveals an identity stronger, more interesting than legal status—more reassuring as well, for the thought of origins soothes us, whereas that of the future disturbs us, agonizes us."[48]

43   Paul Ricoeur, *Time and Narrative*, vol. 3 (Chicago: University of Chicago Press, 1990), 118.

44   Hartman, "Venus in Two Acts," 3.

45   Aline Motta, in the online presentation "Espaço preto (Back Space)," part 2, "Other Foundations?" organized by the Cisneros Institute, The Museum of Modern Art, October 5, 2020. See https://www.moma.org /calendar/events/6706.

46   For more information about Maiolino, see "An Art in Favor of Life: A Conversation with Anna Maria Maiolino," *MoMA Magazine*, February 10, 2022, https://www.moma.org/magazine/articles/693.

47   Roland Barthes, *Camera Lucida: Reflections on Photography* (New York: Hill and Wang, 1981), 103.

48   Barthes, *Camera Lucida*, 105.

49   For a compelling discussion of forgetfulness as a Queer attack on the logic of heteronormative conceptions of time and transmission, see Jack Halberstam, "Dude, Where's My Phallus? Forgetting, Losing, Looping," in *The Queer Art of Failure* (Durham, N.C.: Duke University Press, 2011), 53–86.

But these types of affective bonds are not exclusive to the blood relations associated with heteronormative families.[49] During the final years of the Pinochet regime in Chile, which coincided with the most devastating years of the AIDS crisis, Pedro Lemebel and Francisco Casas, the poetry and performance pair known as Las Yeguas del Apocalipsis, engaged in a regular stream of public actions of resistance against the violent political repression of military dictatorship and in defense of sexual dissidences. In 1989, in a photo studio, they posed together for *Las dos Fridas* (*The Two Fridas*) (1989, plate 63), a direct reference to Frida Kahlo's famous double self-portrait, in which two different images of the artist sit next to each other, holding hands, hearts connected through blood-transfusion tubes. Las Yeguas' image of connection and transmission, viral and loving, expands Kahlo's self-portrait of queerness, mental anguish, and physical suffering into an entirely different context, drawing attention to the medicalization of bodies during the AIDS crisis.

Art outlives us and is, therefore, an instrument for mourning: to film in order to anticipate memory, in the case of Cesarco, or to communicate with the dead, in the case of Nazareth. It also serves to celebrate the fluid ties that connect us with our kinship networks, inherited or chosen—or even to represent processes of forgetting. The work *En Passant* (plate 73), by the Brazilian artist Iran do Espírito Santo, is a perfectly executed series of *degradé* vertical stripes painted on a wall in more than fifty shades of gray. Despite the formal structure of constituent geometric parts, the whole creates an image of fluid continuity reminiscent of the reductive tradition of Minimalism. Yet, in the context of this exhibition, the gradient also serves as a metaphor for the potentially creative effects of forgetfulness.[50]

*

As this account of works in the exhibition outlines, we are currently witnessing a radical reshaping of the notion of art history as a progressive process based on rupture, innovation, and advancement. The critical embrace of longstanding cultural traditions as a way to imagine a common future based on silenced histories that may finally ground us; the opening of the borders of contemporary art to work once seen as belonging in the past or falling outside the value system demarcated by the institutional art world; the challenges that artists have been posing to inherited understandings of landscape, land, and patrimony: all of these developments, in their poetics as well as their politics, are fundamentally transforming previously fixed notions of Latin American contemporary art. The artists here are committed to different modes of retrospection in order to rethink their own narratives, to open them, and through those apertures to change the texture of the present day.

50   About forgetting, Halberstam writes: "We may want to forget family and forget lineage and forget tradition in order to start from a new place, not the place where the old engenders the new, where the old makes a place for the new, but where the new begins afresh, unfettered by memory, traditions and usable pasts." Halberstam, *The Queer Art of Failure*, 70.

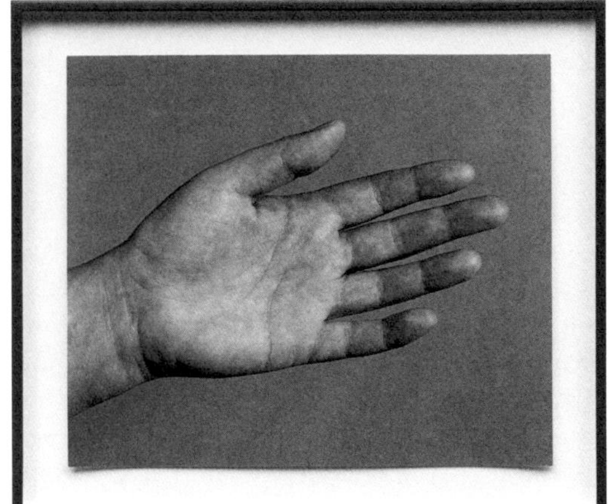

Plate 56

Alejandro Cesarco (Uruguayan, born 1975)
Studies for a Series on Love (Wendy's Hands). 2015
Archival inkjet print, framed
10 7/16 × 12 3/16" (26.5 × 31 cm)
Collection the artist

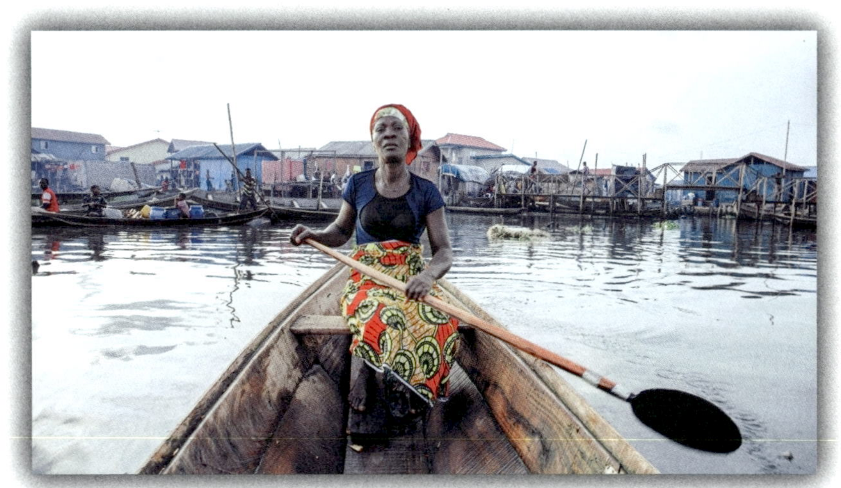

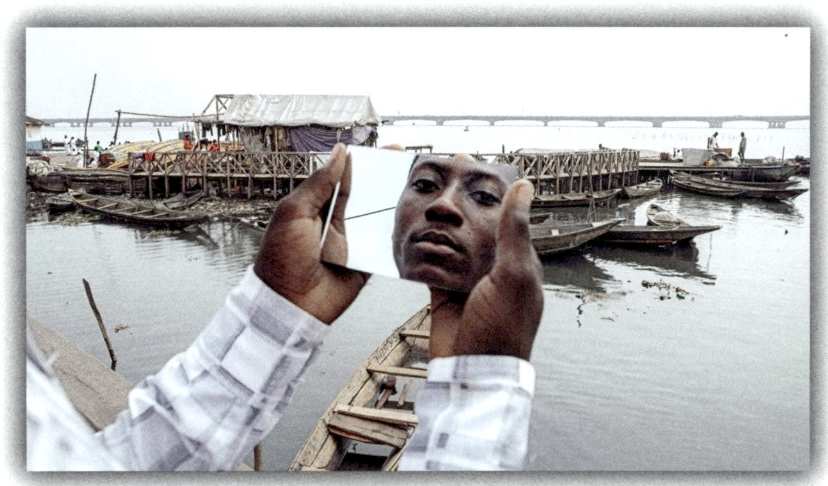

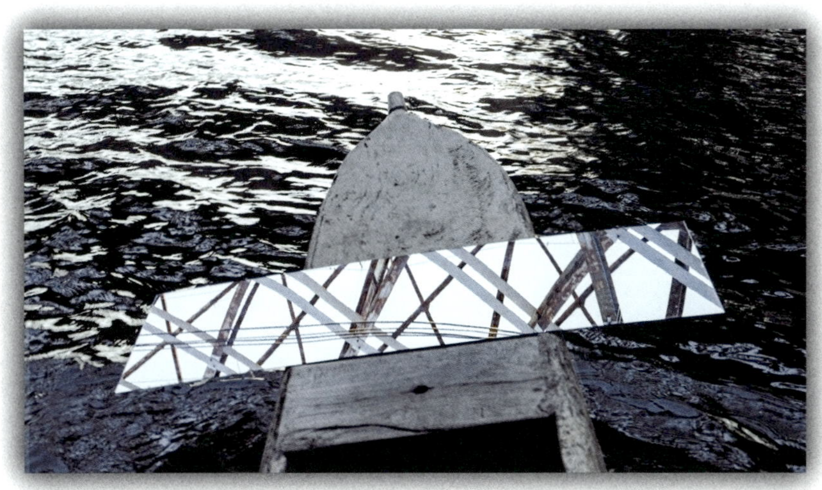

Plates 57–59

Aline Motta (Brazilian, born 1974)
(Outros) Fundamentos ([*Other*] *Foundations)*. 2017–19
Video (color, sound), 15:48 min.

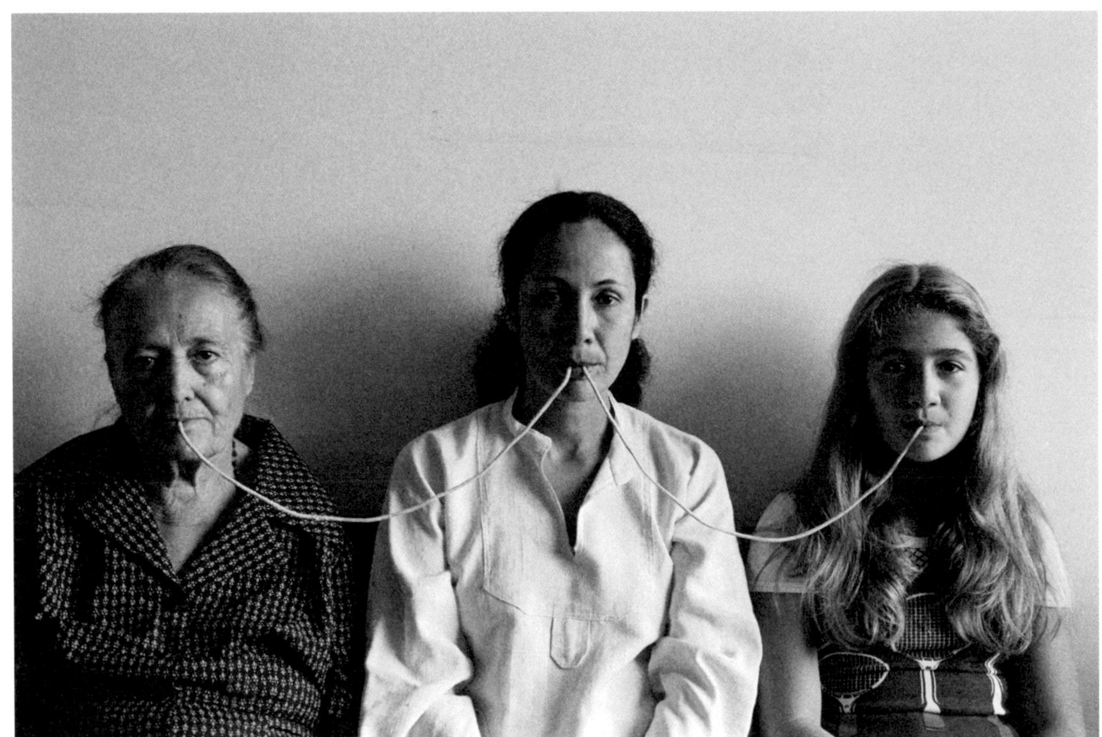

Plate 60

Anna Maria Maiolino (Brazilian, born Italy 1942)
Por um fio (*By a Thread*), from Fotopoemação (Photopoemaction). 1976/2017
Black-and-white inkjet print
20 ½ × 31 ⅛" (52 × 79 cm)
Collection the artist and Hauser & Wirth

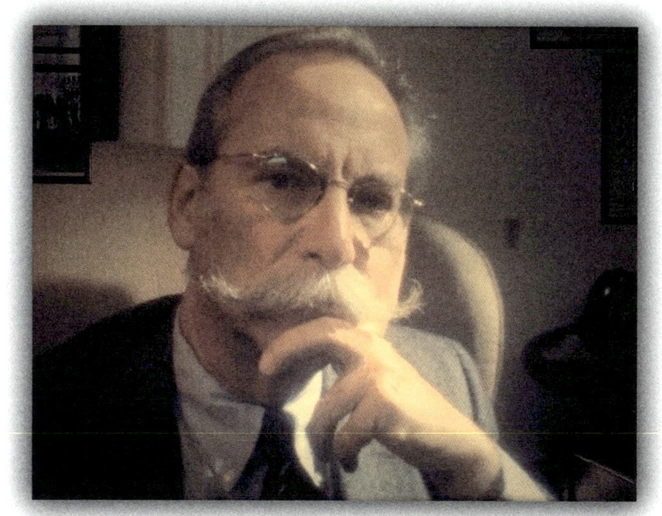

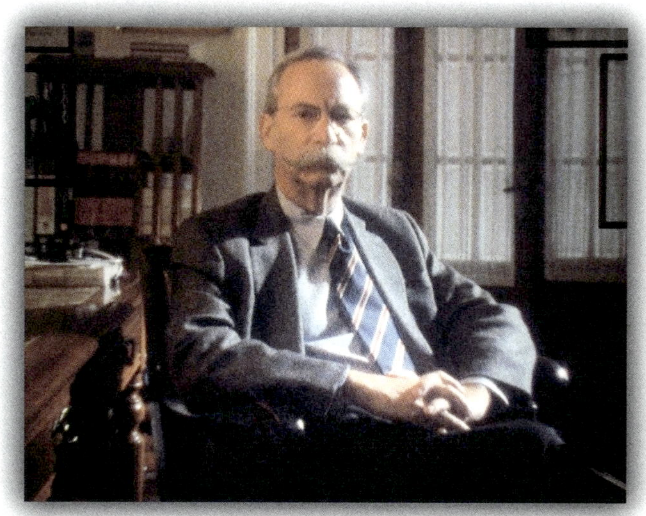

Plates 61, 62

Alejandro Cesarco (Uruguayan, born 1975)
Present Memory. 2009
Video (color, silent), 3 min.

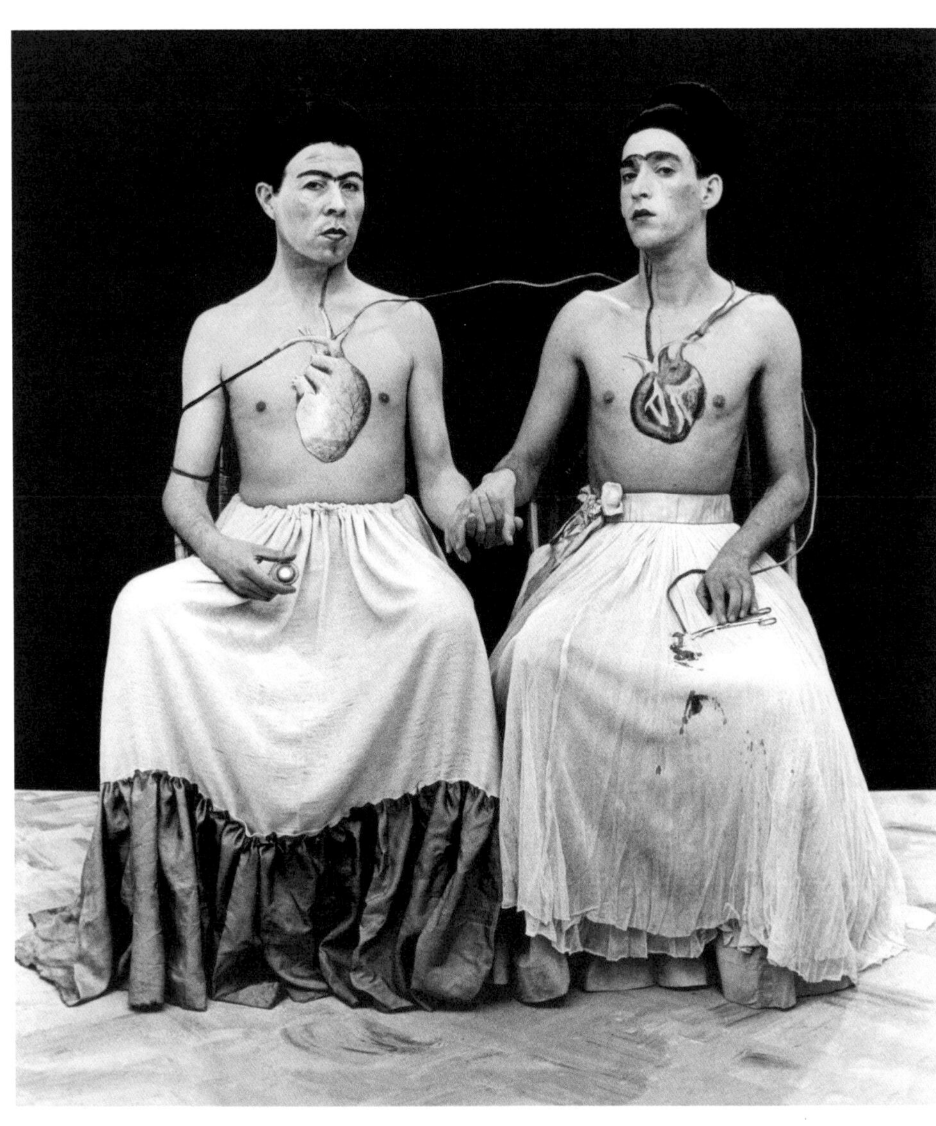

Plate 63

Las Yeguas del Apocalipsis (Chilean, 1987–1997)
Pedro Mardones Lemebel (Chilean, 1952–2015)
and Francisco Casas Silva (Chilean, born 1959)
Las dos Fridas (*The Two Fridas*). 1989
Inkjet print
49 ³⁄₁₆ × 47 ¼" (125 × 120 cm)

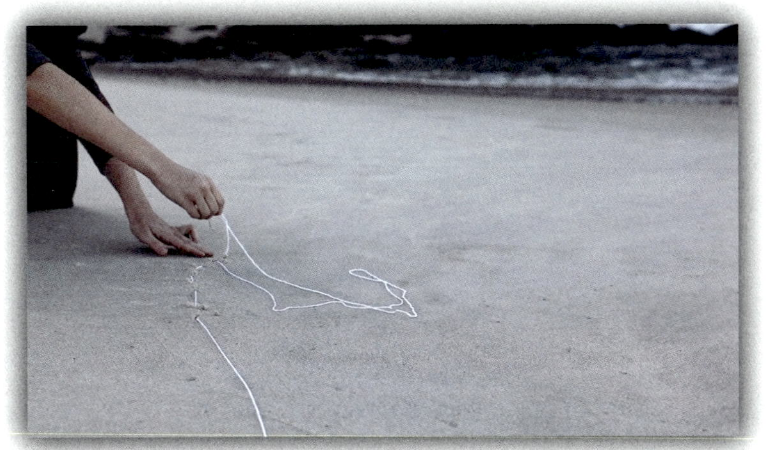

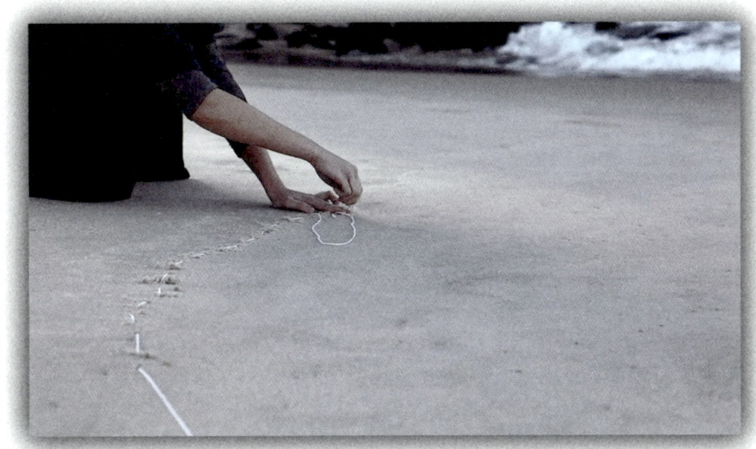

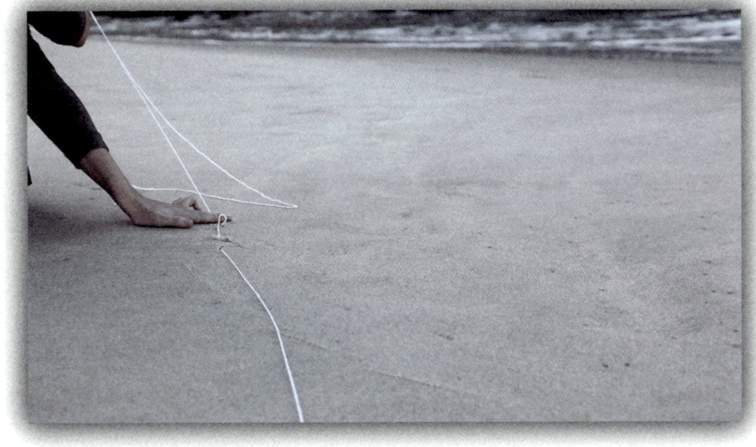

Plates 64–66

Maria Laet (Brazilian, born 1982)
Notas sobre o limite do mar (*Notes on the Limit of the Sea*). 2011
Video (color, silent), 11:42 min

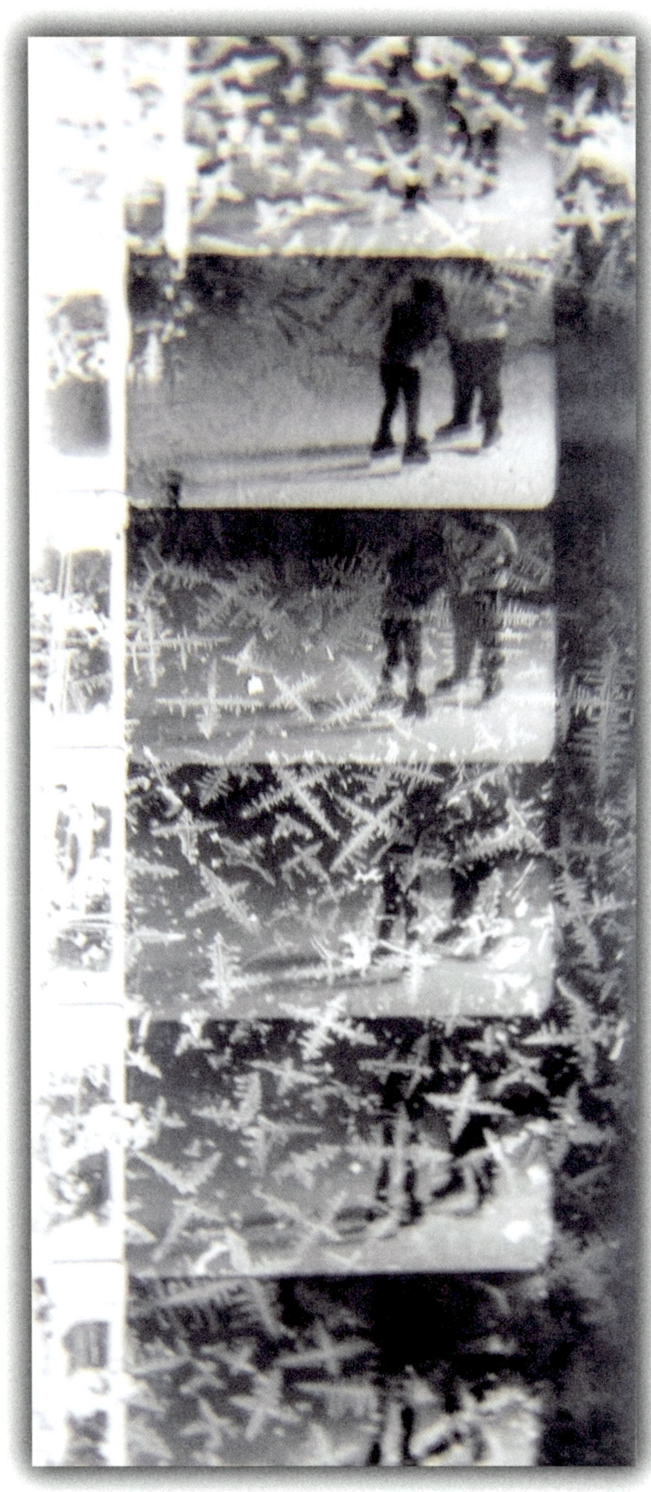

Plate 67

Sofía Gallisá Muriente (Puerto Rican, born 1986)
Asimilar y destruir (Assimilate and Destroy). 2019
16mm film transferred to video (black and white, silent), 2:38 min.

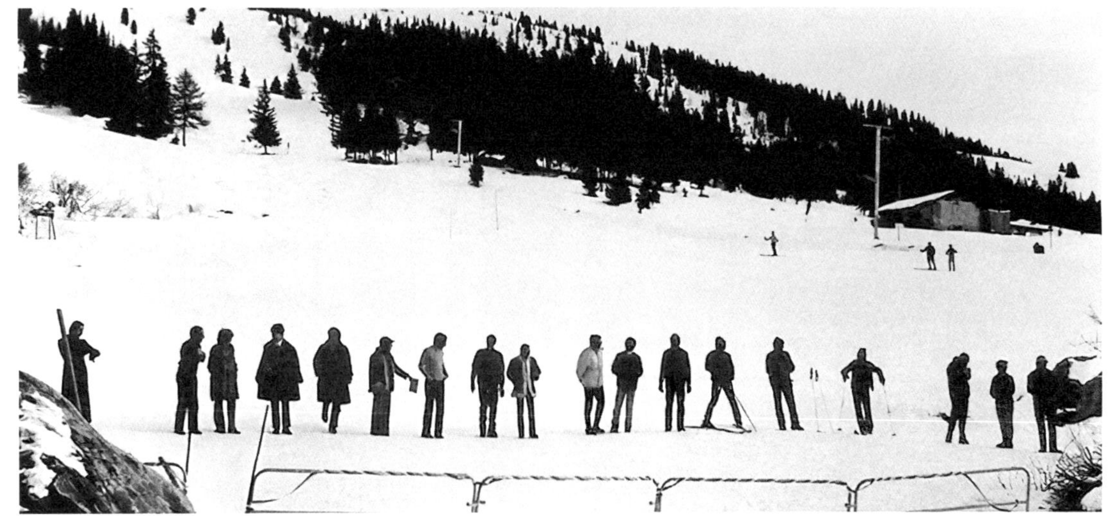

Plate 68

David Lamelas (Argentine, born 1946)
Time. 1970
Gelatin silver print
9 1/16 × 22 5/16" (23 × 56.7 cm)

91

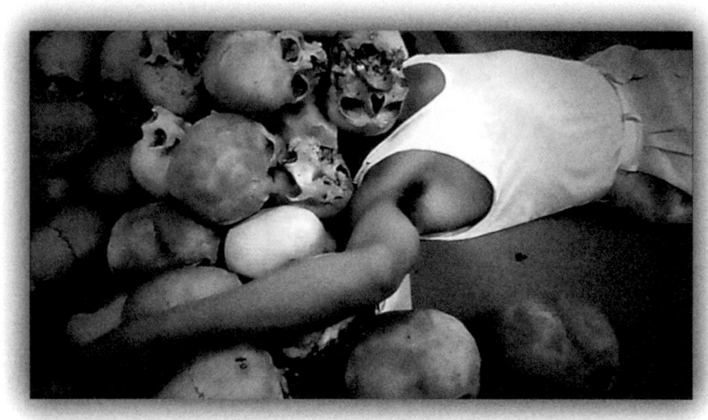

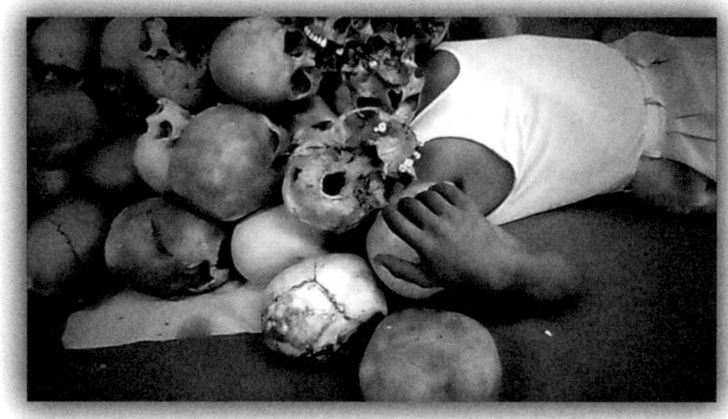

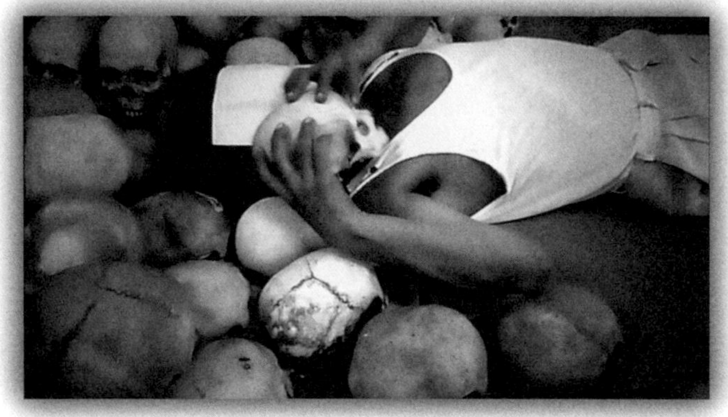

Plates 69–71

Paulo Nazareth (Brazilian, born 1977)
Antropologia do negro II (*Black Anthropology II*). 2014
High-definition video (black and white, sound), 7:21 min

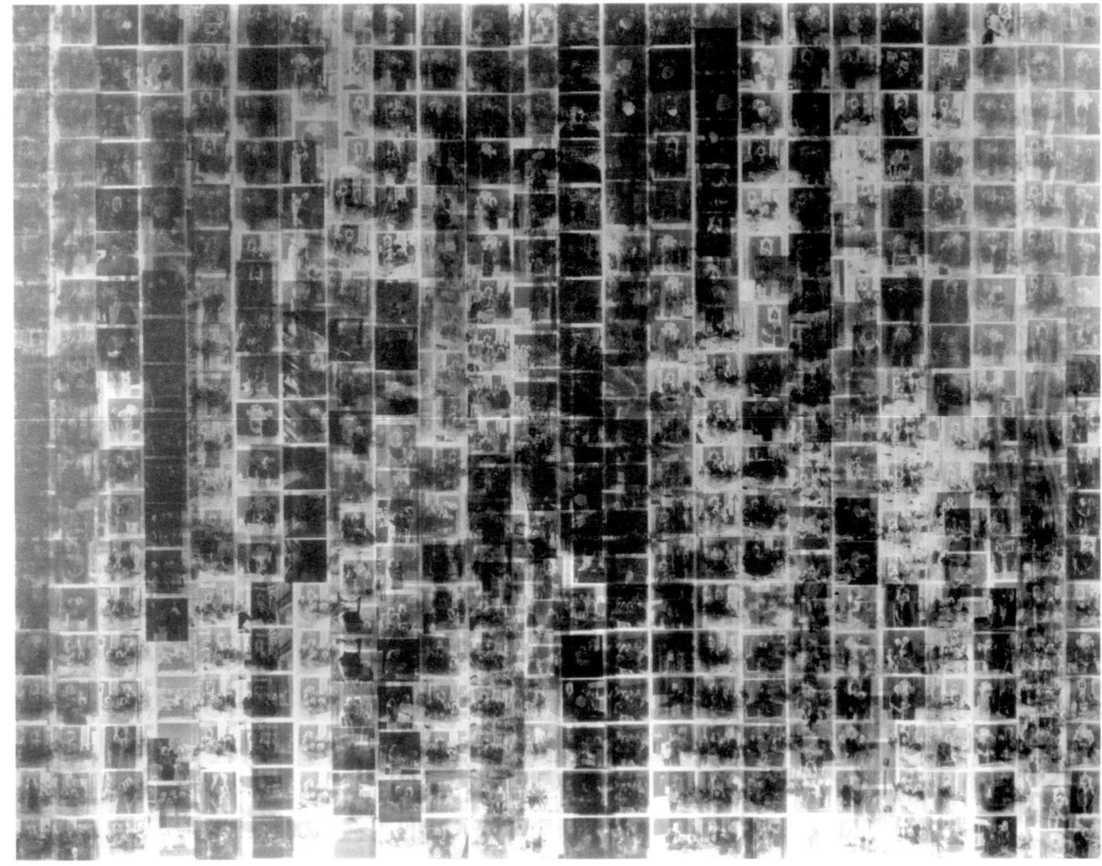

Rosângela Rennó (Brazilian, born 1962)
Wedding Landscape. 1996
Gelatin silver negatives and acrylic
44 ¾ × 58 ½ × ½" (113.7 × 148.6 × 1.3 cm)

93

III

Iran do Espírito Santo (Brazilian, born 1963)
En Passant. 2008
Site-specific wall painting, installation view,
Galeria Fortes Vilaça, São Paulo, 2008
Collection the artist

94

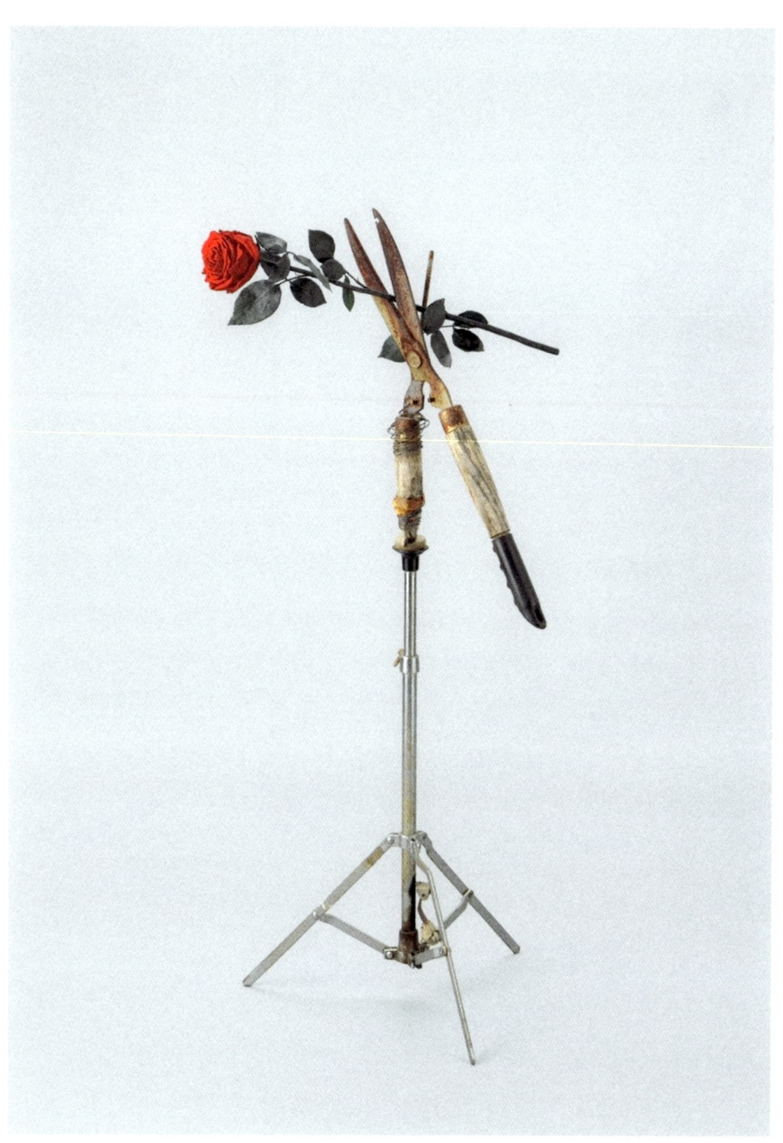

Plate 74

Claudio Perna (Venezuelan, born Italy. 1938–1997)
Haute Couture. 1967–68
Metal stand, garden shears, wire, felt, rubber, and rose
47 ⅛ × 11 ½ × 9 ⅛" (119.5 × 29 × 23 cm)

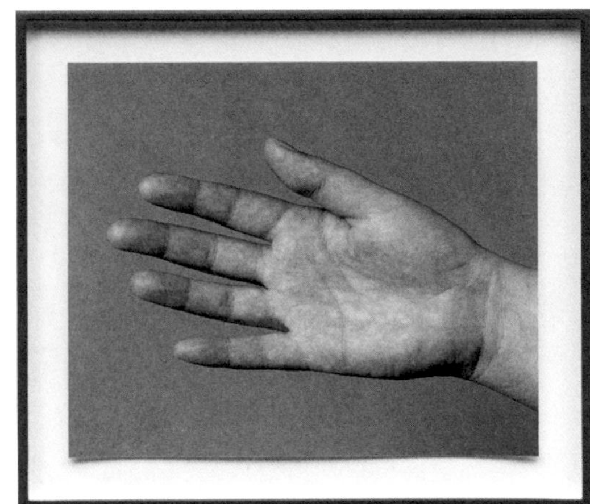

Plate 75

Alejandro Cesarco (Uruguayan, born 1975)
Studies for a Series on Love (Wendy's Hands). 2015
Archival inkjet print, framed
10 ⁷⁄₁₆ × 12 ³⁄₁₆" (26.5 × 31 cm)
Collection the artist

IN DIALOGUE

A Brief History of the Colección Patricia Phelps
de Cisneros and the Latin American Collection
at The Museum of Modern Art

JULIA DETCHON

Latin American art has always been an integral part of The Museum of Modern Art's story of modernism, although its place in the collection and exhibition program has often depended on the enthusiasm of its champions, both within the Museum and without, over the years. In the last four decades, MoMA's collection of Latin American works has been shaped, in large part, by the vision and generosity of Trustee Patricia Phelps de Cisneros together with the strong support of Director Glenn D. Lowry. The present exhibition celebrates Cisneros's gift of contemporary works that enrich the Museum's holdings and open up new connections among the represented artists, many of whom are entering the collection for the first time.

This gift of contemporary art is by no means Cisneros's first to the Museum. It follows a major gift, in 2016, of more than one hundred paintings, sculptures, and works on paper by artists working in mid-century Argentina, Brazil, Uruguay, and Venezuela. While they entered the Museum's collection separately, the Modern and Contemporary Gifts have always existed in dialogue—with each other, with the other collecting areas of the Colección Patricia Phelps de Cisneros, and with the many works Cisneros had funded and donated earlier. Indeed, Cisneros's gifts tell a story not only of her astute collecting and transformative generosity but also of a sustained dialogue between institutions over decades—one that has changed the historical narrative of Latin American art at MoMA and around the world.

LATIN AMERICAN ART AT MOMA

In 1931, just two years after MoMA's founding, Diego Rivera was the focus of its second solo exhibition, and four years later, the acquisition of José Clemente Orozco's painting *The Subway* (1928) and Rivera's sketchbook *May Day, Moscow* (1928) initiated the Museum's collection of works by Latin American artists. The collection expanded in 1942 thanks to the Inter-American Fund, established by a donation from Nelson Rockefeller, MoMA's former president and coordinator of the U.S. government's recently created Office of Inter-American Affairs (OIAA). The Inter-American Fund's overt purpose—to fund purchases of Latin American art for the Museum's collection—dovetailed with a more covert set of interests on the part of the OIAA, which sought to track and block Axis influence in the Western Hemisphere through cultural patronage. It was with this dual mission that MoMA dispatched Lincoln Kirstein, who had been named "Consultant on Latin-American Art," on a collecting trip to South America in 1942.[1]

Traveling to Brazil, Argentina, Uruguay, Chile, Peru, Ecuador, Colombia, and Mexico, Kirstein acquired 141 works, which, combined with acquisitions made by Director Alfred H. Barr, Jr., in Mexico and Cuba that summer, more than tripled the size of the Latin American collection. Upon Kirstein's return to New York, he proposed the creation of a department of Latin American art at MoMA. Although the idea did not come to fruition, his acquisitions were highlighted in

1   See Gabriel Pérez-Barreiro, "The Accidental Tourist: American Collections of Latin American Art," in *Collecting the New: Museums and Contemporary Art*, ed. Bruce Altshuler (Princeton, N.J.: Princeton University Press, 2007), 131–46; Miriam Basilio, "Reflecting on a History of Collecting and Exhibiting Work by Artists from Latin America," in *MoMA at El Museo: Latin American and Caribbean Art from the Collection of The Museum of Modern Art* (New York: El Museo del Barrio and The Museum of Modern Art, 2004), 52–63; and, more recently, Michele Greet, "Looking South: Lincoln Kirstein and Latin American Art," in *Lincoln Kirstein's Modern*, ed. Samantha Friedman and Jodi Hauptman (New York: The Museum of Modern Art, 2019), 144–53. See also John Elderfield, "The Geometry of Change," in *A Constructive Vision: Latin American Art from the Colección Patricia Phelps de Cisneros* (New York: Fundación Cisneros, 2010), 26.

The Latin-American Collection of the Museum of Modern Art (March–June 1943), the Museum's first survey of Latin American art (fig. 1). However, Kirstein's selections, as art historian Michele Greet notes, "were out of keeping with what would prove to be the dominant trends in modernism," trends established by major exhibitions of abstract art organized by the Museum in the next decade.[2] The disjunction between the figurative and regionalist works Kirstein purchased and the more experimental formalism championed in the following years suggests a certain irony embedded in MoMA's collecting history: that the personal taste of its earliest Latin American specialist may have contributed to a persistent sense that the region was not sufficiently modern.

Fig. 1   Exhibition catalogue for *The Latin-American Collection of the Museum of Modern Art*, by Lincoln Kirstein (New York: The Museum of Modern Art, 1943)

Fig. 2   Installation view of the exhibition *Latin American Artists of the Twentieth Century*, The Museum of Modern Art, New York, 1993

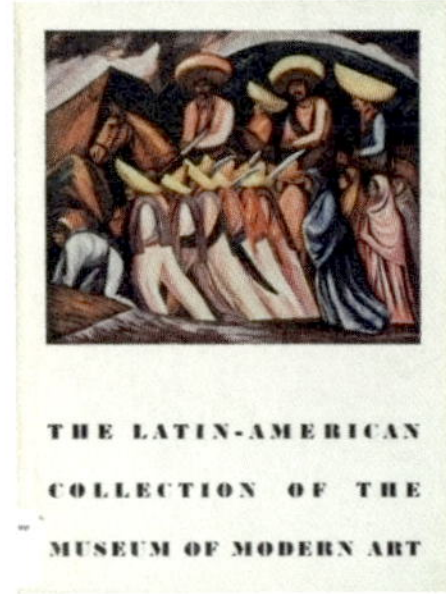

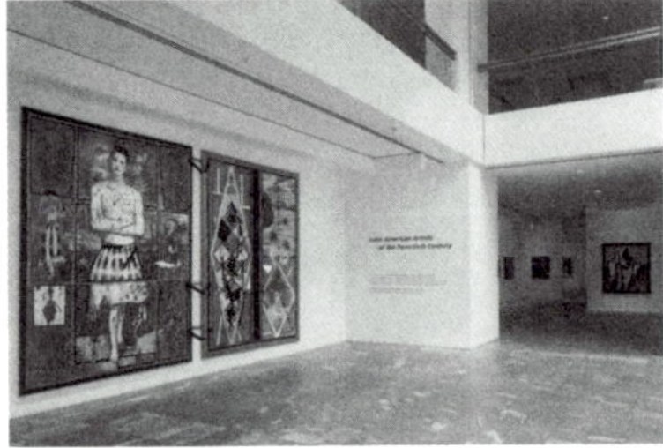

Rockefeller's vision of modern art as cultural diplomacy was formalized with the establishment of the Museum's International Program in 1952. Throughout the 1950s and 1960s, the program circulated popular exhibitions such as Edward Steichen's *The Family of Man* in Central and South America and organized United States representation in the newly established São Paulo Biennial. In 1970–74, the International Council, which provides long-term financial support for the program, was chaired by Alfredo Boulton, a Venezuelan art historian, collector, and photographer. In the early 1980s, Boulton's grandniece, Patricia Phelps de Cisneros, joined a museum-organized trip to Brazil and, later, the International Council.

If the Museum's interest in collecting Latin American art during these years was sporadic at best, through the International Program, Kirstein's vision for exhibitions focused on the region lived on. In 1992, fifty years after Kirstein's journey, the program's director, Waldo Rasmussen, organized the survey *Latin American Artists of the Twentieth Century*, which opened at the Plaza de Armas in Seville and toured in Europe before closing in New York the following year (fig. 2). Coinciding with the quincentenary of the arrival of Europeans in the Americas, the survey was criticized in part for taking a totalizing view of the region. The debates surrounding this show revealed some of the historical links between MoMA's collecting practices, exhibition programs, and political imperatives—and the need for revision. Nevertheless, the exhibition was a turning point for Cisneros. "The show needed funds," she remembers, "and I didn't know anything about fundraising but I wanted to help."[3] Cisneros undertook her first dedicated fundraising effort for the Museum, a task she later compared to crowdfunding, and the catalogue notes that the exhibition was "made possible by grants from Mr. and Mrs. Gustavo Cisneros."[4]

THE COLECCIÓN PATRICIA PHELPS DE CISNEROS

Two decades earlier, Patricia Phelps de Cisneros had begun assembling a collection in Caracas with her husband, Gustavo A. Cisneros.[5] Having grown up amid the efflorescence of modernist architecture in Caracas—embodied best,

2   Greet, "Looking South," 146.

3   Glenn D. Lowry, "An Interview with Patricia Phelps de Cisneros," in *Sur moderno: Journeys of Abstraction—The Patricia Phelps de Cisneros Gift*, ed. Inés Katzenstein and María Amalia García (New York: The Museum of Modern Art, 2019), 19.

4   Waldo Rasmussen, ed., *Latin American Artists of the Twentieth Century* (New York: The Museum of Modern Art, 1992).

5   Curator Ariel Jiménez writes about the significance of Caracas in the conception of the CPPC in "The Colección Patricia Phelps de Cisneros: The Evolution of a Collection," in *A Constructive Vision*, 64–85.

perhaps, by Carlos Raúl Villanueva's Ciudad Universitaria, which integrates works by Wifredo Lam, Alejandro Otero, Jesús Rafael Soto, Jean Arp, and Alexander Calder, among others, into its utopian plan—she developed an enthusiasm for kinetic and geometric abstraction that was nurtured by conversations with Sofía Ímber, a curator and patron who had recently founded the Caracas Museum of Contemporary Art.[6]

As Cisneros told James Cuno years later, "Sofía's museum would bring artists from [other South American countries] to Venezuela, and Gustavo's determination to look outside of Venezuela, to look beyond the local, inspired me to research art from elsewhere in Latin America."[7] Her interest in abstraction led Patricia and Gustavo to collect thematically across the region, assembling a transnational history of mid-century geometric abstraction in Latin America that ultimately included chapters on Concrete, Neo-Concrete, and Kinetic movements emanating from metropolitan centers like Buenos Aires, Montevideo, Rio de Janeiro, São Paulo, and Caracas (fig. 3).[8] These were among the same cities Kirstein had visited, now telling a very different story.

Fig. 3   Patricia Phelps de Cisneros with a work by Leda Catunda at Galeria Fortes Vilaça, São Paulo, 1996

Fig. 4   Patricia Phelps de Cisneros and her daughter Adriana in the studio of Eduardo Ramírez Villamizar, Bogotá, 1991

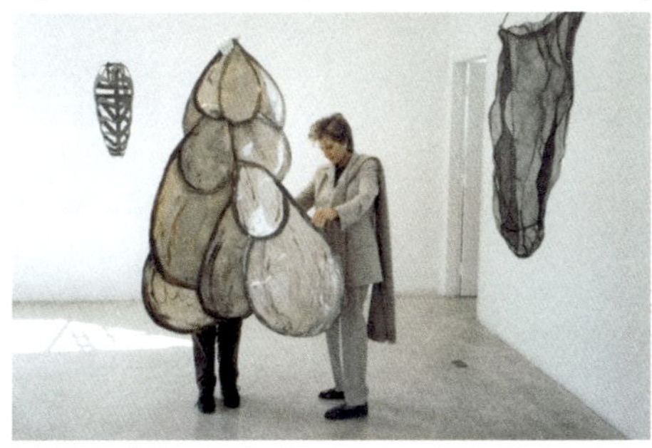

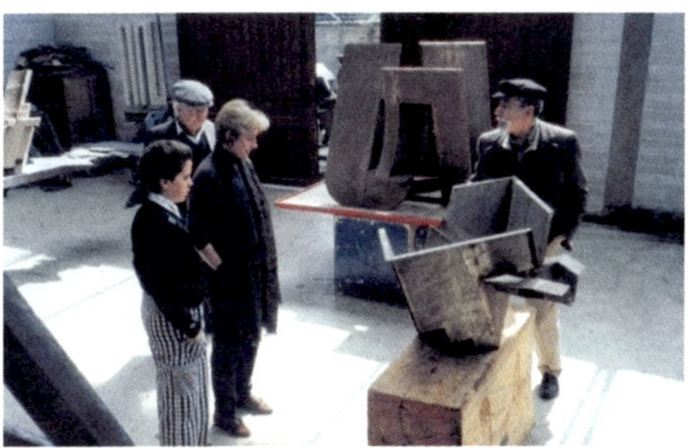

What became known, in the 1990s, as the Colección Patricia Phelps de Cisneros (CPPC) expanded to encompass five distinct collecting areas: modern and contemporary art from Latin America; artworks and documentation by traveler artists to and within Latin America and the Caribbean from the seventeenth to nineteenth centuries; furniture, art, and objects from Latin America's colonial period; and art and artifacts from Indigenous peoples of the Orinoco River basin in the Venezuelan Amazon. Venezuelan art historian Luis Pérez-Oramas became curator of the Colección in 1995 and was soon joined by Paulo Herkenhoff, Ariel Jiménez, and Rafael Romero, former director of the Galería de Arte Nacional in Venezuela, all of whom focused on the modern, contemporary, and landscape collections. Curator Jorge Rivas Pérez focused on building the collection of art and objects from the colonial period, and Lelia Delgado, Andrés Ortega, and Zuleima Jiménez focused on the Orinoco holdings.[9]

Cisneros often describes the sense of responsibility that grew with her collection as it developed. "In fact," she has written, "you have a long list of responsibilities: to safeguard and conserve the work; to archive it; to learn as much as you can about it; to share it; and to create the proper conditions for scholarship that will elucidate the works and their relationship within a larger cultural context."[10] Patricia, Gustavo, and their children Guillermo, Carolina, and Adriana

<hr>

6   Lowry, "An Interview with Patricia Phelps de Cisneros," 22.

7   James Cuno, "A Conversation with Patricia Phelps de Cisneros," in *A Constructive Vision*, 17.

8   See Gabriel Pérez-Barreiro, *The Geometry of Hope: Latin American Abstract Art from the Patricia Phelps de Cisneros Collection* (Austin: Blanton Museum of Art, University of Texas at Austin, 2007).

9   Thomas Ammann and Rafael Pereira played important roles in the early days of the CPPC, and Jorge Rivas, Andrés Ortega, and Zuleima Jiménez were crucial in its growth. See Ariel Jiménez, "The Colección Patricia Phelps de Cisneros," for discussion of this transition to the CPPC's "mature period."

10   Patricia Phelps de Cisneros, "Private Collections: To Build or Not to Build?" in *Debates: A Public Forum on Issues Shaping the Field*, https://www.coleccioncisneros.org/editorial/debate/private-collections-build-or-not-build (archived editorial platform of the Cisneros collection), accessed August 5, 2022. The CPPC has supported scholarship in the form of a robust program of publications, including exhibition catalogues, monographs, and the bilingual *Conversaciones/Conversations* series.

101

made the choice not to build a private museum to house the collection, a somewhat unusual decision given the role private museums were playing in the development of a globalized arts infrastructure throughout Latin America at the time. "Instead of putting our efforts into creating a museum," Cisneros explained, "we felt very strongly that it was important to circulate the works in our care—the majority of which were little known when we acquired them—through vigorous lending so that they could be seen internationally and in a wide variety of contexts."[11] And lend vigorously they did. The collection of geometric abstraction, in particular, circulated extensively not only in Latin America but also in the United States, Europe, Japan, and China. Cisneros summarized her goals in a presentation to ARCO Madrid in 1997: "This is where I see my responsibility as a collector of modern and contemporary Latin American art: to contribute to projecting the marvelous creative complexity of our continent . . . which, without ceasing to be very much ours, is fully universal."[12]

That year, with the goal of integrating Latin American art into public collections, the Colección Cisneros began donating works to institutions in the United States, Europe, Venezuela, Peru, and Argentina. During MoMA's renovation in 2002–04, Cisneros invited John Elderfield, at that time the Marie-Josée and Henry Kravis Chief Curator of Painting and Sculpture, to work with Pérez-Oramas, then an adjunct curator at MoMA, to select works from her collection that would improve the Museum's Latin American holdings. "We soon concluded that we needed to acquire works from the Argentine Arte Concreto-Invención and Madí movements, and Brazilian Concretism and Neoconcretism, as well as by early modernists in Venezuela and Uruguay," Elderfield recalled. "And that was just for a start."[13] While the Colección Cisneros's acquisitions, particularly under Jiménez, underscored the dialogue between Latin American artists and their counterparts in the United States (Josef Albers, Alexander Calder) and Europe (Piet Mondrian, Max Bill), Elderfield's selections brought this dialogue into the Museum's galleries. The Museum's reinstallation grouped paintings by Joaquin Torres-García with those of Mondrian (fig. 7) and works by Alejandro Otero with those of Albers and Robert Motherwell. "In a certain sense," Jiménez writes, "Cisneros's work as a collector found an institutional equivalent at MoMA."[14]

Cisneros's strategic gifts and traveling exhibitions made a profound impact on presentations of modern art not just at MoMA but also at other institutions around the United States. If folkloric techniques or social realist narratives characterized art from the region as it was historically collected, the Colección Cisneros shifted the emphasis toward geometric abstraction, integrating Latin American movements into international histories of modernism. As Elderfield wrote, "It was the exclusion of geometric abstraction from the history of the region's art that sustained its marginalization or glamorization, or both, as an art of the fantastic, separate from international modernism—as well as the generalization of fantastic art, and other Latin American forms of realism, in support of this separation."[15]

11 Cisneros, "Private Collections: To Build or Not to Build?"

12 Patricia Phelps de Cisneros, *Coleccionar en américa latina* (Venezuela: Colección Patricia Phelps de Cisneros, 1997), 16. Among the many exhibitions organized with the CPPC's collection are *Geometric Abstraction* (Fogg Art Museum, 2001), *The Geometry of Hope* (Blanton Museum of Art, 2007), *Concrete Invention* (Museo Reina Sofía, 2013), and *Making Art Concrete* (Getty Research Institute, 2017).

13 Elderfield, "The Geometry of Change," 25.

14 Jiménez, "The Colección Patricia Phelps de Cisneros," 80.

15 Elderfield, "The Geometry of Change," 25

The balance has tipped such that presentations of Latin American art must attend to the integral role of geometric abstraction from the region as one of the pillars of art in the twentieth century. "I do feel it is 'mission accomplished' in some ways," Cisneros has said.[16]

THE MOMA GIFT

Cisneros became a trustee of the Museum in 1992. In addition to germinal gifts of forty works of art before the Modern Gift in 2016, her early collaborations with the Museum included establishing the Cisneros Travel Fund, for curators to see Latin American art firsthand, and the Cisneros Bibliographer for Latin America. Both led to important acquisitions; the first travel grant, given to then-Associate Curator of Architecture and Design Paola Antonelli, resulted in the 1998 *Projects 66* exhibition of Brazilian designers Fernando and Humberto Campana, whose innovative furniture entered the collection through early Cisneros gifts. In 2006, Cisneros formalized the acquisition of art from Latin America by founding the Latin American and Caribbean Fund, a "vigorous mechanism for funding acquisitions" which has, to date, added over 1,200 works from the region to MoMA's collection.[17] In addition, these programs have supported programming, education, conservation, exhibitions, and publications. One such publication was *Alfredo Boulton and His Contemporaries: Critical Dialogues in Venezuelan Art, 1912–1974*, edited by Jiménez as part of a series of documentary anthologies produced by the International Program (fig. 5).[18] A series of seminars co-organized by the Colección Cisneros and the International Program brought conservation, collection management, curatorial, and education teams to Caracas, fostering institutional exchange.

Educational programs opened up new avenues for dialogue; if the role of Latin American art at MoMA was, in its early days, bound up with Nelson Rockefeller's vision of modern art as cultural diplomacy, its promotion by Cisneros was increasingly tied to a "politics" rooted in scholarly exchange. Inspired by the pedagogical values of the Visual Thinking Curriculum, a school-based program developed by the Museum's Department of Education which she first encountered on a visit to the 1997 survey of Manuel Álvarez Bravo, the Colección Cisneros created an expansive educational program of its own. Piensa en Arte/Think Art, as it was known, was implemented first through the Galería de Arte Nacional in Venezuela and later in seven countries. In addition to drawing from MoMA's models in its activities around the world, Cisneros's commitment to research on Latin American art—from contextualizing the works in her collection to funding academic programs at universities—would later take shape in the form of a dedicated research center at the Museum.

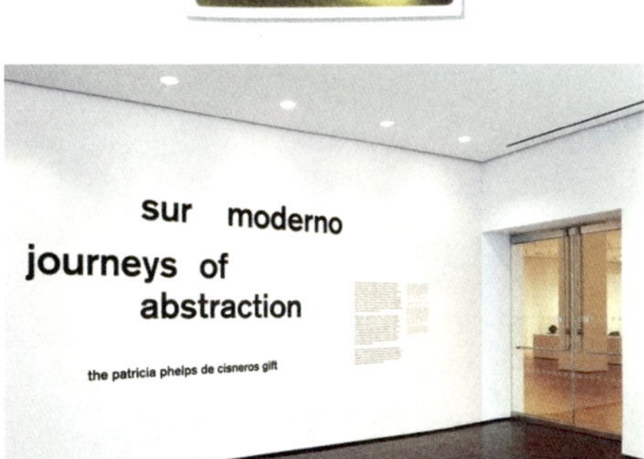

Fig. 5   Ariel Jiménez, *Alfredo Boulton and His Contemporaries: Critical Dialogues in Venezuelan Art, 1912-1974* (New York: The Museum of Modern Art, 2008)

Fig. 6   Entrance to the exhibition *Sur moderno: Journeys of Abstraction—The Patricia Phelps de Cisneros Gift*, The Museum of Modern Art, New York, 2019

Cisneros's donations culminated in October 2016 with the transformative gift of 102 works by pioneering artists from mid-century Latin America. The gift also built on prior institutional collaborations by endowing the Patricia Phelps de Cisneros Research Institute for the Study of Art from Latin America, an ambitious platform dedicated to stimulating, supporting, and disseminating

16   Lowry, "An Interview with Patricia Phelps de Cisneros," 23.

17   Unpublished mission statement, 2006, Latin American and Caribbean Fund files, The Museum of Modern Art, New York.

18   See Ariel Jiménez, ed., *Alfredo Boulton and His Contemporaries: Critical Dialogues in Venezuelan Art, 1912-1974* (New York: The Museum of Modern Art, 2008).

new understandings of Latin American modern and contemporary art in relationship to broader cultural issues within a global context. Cisneros credits the "brilliant guidance and friendship" of Elderfield, who, in addition to making early selections, advised on the formation of a research center to support them, with this major donation.

The Modern Gift was celebrated in the 2019 exhibition *Sur moderno: Journeys of Abstraction—The Patricia Phelps de Cisneros Gift*, a comprehensive look at the ways that South American artists revolutionized painting, sculpture, design, and architecture at mid-century (fig. 6). The exhibition was organized by Inés Katzenstein, Curator of Latin American Art and the inaugural director of the Research Institute, and consulting curator María Amalia García, Consejo Nacional de Investigaciones Científicas y Técnicas–Universidad Nacional de San Martín, with Karen Grimson, Curatorial Assistant, Department of Drawings and Prints.

The Modern Gift has also played a major role in the revised presentation of the Museum's collection since it reopened, again, in 2019. Works originating from the Colección Cisneros are integrated into the regularly rotating chronological, geographic, and thematic galleries dedicated to the Museum's permanent collection, forming the basis for an installation that is both more international and more contextual (fig. 8). But the space for revision opened up by this gift did not close at mid-century. As Cisneros reflected, "A fertile ground has been built for the contemporary, for the work of the youngest masters, in which various artistic legacies—the structural, the pictorial, and the social—intersect without contradictions."[19]

Fig. 7   Installation view of the gallery "Circle and Square: Joaquin Torres-Garcia and Piet Mondrian," The Museum of Modern Art, New York, 2020

Fig. 8   Installation view of works by Mira Schendel, Lygia Clark, Agnes Martin, and Gego (Gertrud Goldschmidt) in the gallery "Touching the Void," The Museum of Modern Art, New York, 2020

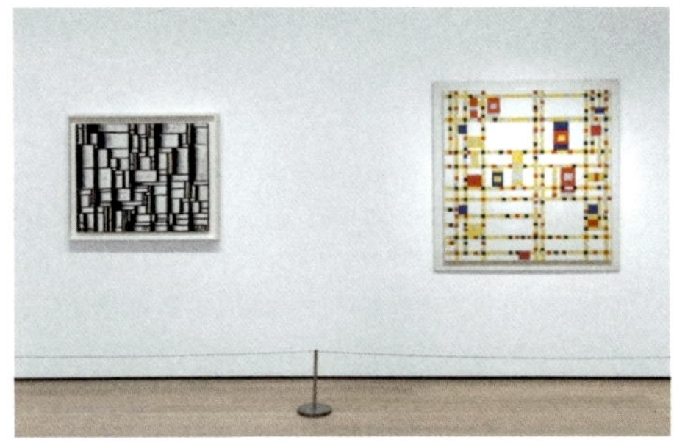

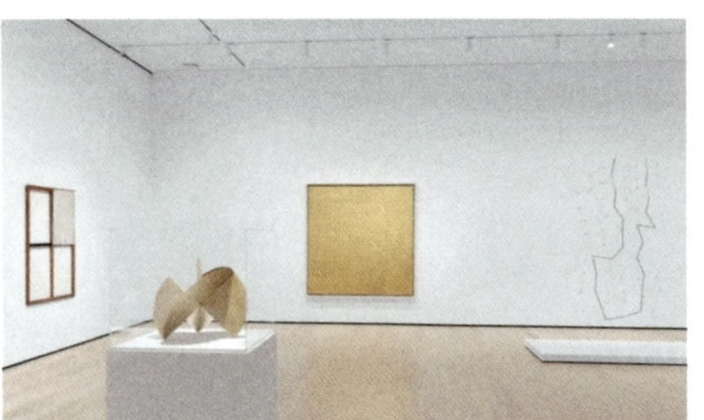

COLLECTING CONTEMPORARY

As curators of the Colección Cisneros are quick to point out, collecting choices have always been shaped by Cisneros herself, in tandem with advisers and specialists in modern and contemporary art, such as Rafael Pereira, Paulo Herkenhoff, Luis Pérez-Oramas, Ariel Jiménez, Gabriel Pérez-Barreiro, and Sofía Hernández Chong Cuy. Cisneros regularly visits artists in their studios and often traveled with Colección curators to stay abreast of new work from Latin America and to see potential acquisitions in person. Indeed, Cisneros's interests have been "contemporary" from the start; even the "modern" works were contemporary at their time of purchase. But former director Pérez-Barreiro notes that it was during the 1990s, when the collection was institutionalized as a project of international scope, that a specifically contemporary strategy was outlined in response to the existing collecting areas. That strategy, Cisneros notes, developed with institutional giving in mind: "I would not do anything without consulting with John Elderfield and Gabriel Pérez-Barreiro," she says, always considering how additions to her collection would impact public collections in the future—not only in New York but also internationally, thanks to Pérez-Barreiro's involvement.[20]

19   Cisneros, *Coleccionar en américa latina*, 25.

20   Interview with the author, October 25, 2022.

21   Lowry, "Interview with Patricia Phelps de Cisneros," 22.

22   Luis Pérez-Oramas, *Arte contemporáneo venezolano en la Colección Cisneros: 1990–2004* (Caracas: Fundación Cisneros, 2005), 24.

Herkenhoff, a close adviser and curator of the groundbreaking 1998 São Paulo Biennial, introduced, in addition to the Concrete and Neo-Concrete pioneers, contemporary Brazilian artists such as Cildo Meireles, Waltercio Caldas, and Jac Leirner. "Paulo Herkenhoff, together with Gustavo, actually made me aware that there was a bigger world out there that needed to be paid attention to," Cisneros recalled in an interview with Lowry. "Paulo taught me to look not just at Latin American art, but at art in general."[21] Acquisitions proposed by Pérez-Oramas and Jiménez likewise highlighted the relationships between Venezuelan modernism and contemporary responses by Claudio Perna, Eugenio Espinosa, and Héctor Fuenmayor, among others. "What remains of Otero in the painting of our time?" Pérez-Oramas asked in a 2004 presentation that anticipated the themes of the contemporary collection.[22] Revisions of the utopian promises of modernism, of the pictorial fictions of landscape, of the formal history of the monochrome and the relationship between nature and abstraction: these are all points of contact and ongoing processes that breach the fugitive temporal divide between the modern and the contemporary.

An exemplary figure in these processes, for Pérez-Oramas, was Roberto Obregón, whose meticulous deconstructions of nature turned away from the monumental thinking of the mid-century masters. Obregón's painting *ADM* (1978–90, plate 35), elegiac in its typological arrangement of the petals of a single rose, marks time during a period when the political promise embedded in institutionalized forms, such as kinetic and geometric abstraction, was revealed to be precarious. "A bit like Otero of the 1940s, authoring, from paintings full of absence, the practice of a new abstract freedom, Obregón inaugurates a new artistic option for nature," Pérez-Oramas writes, threading lines of continuity in the "artifices and tricks" of a more postmodern view of the past.[23] It is a stance shared by other artists of this transitional moment, such as Waltercio Caldas, whose *Painted Iron* (1978) appears, at first glance, to be engaged with the language of geometric abstraction (fig. 9). And yet, the reference is also to the spatial composition of a genre scene by Velázquez, a reflection on the nature of representation in the Western tradition.[24]

Obregón, Caldas, and the Contemporary Gift broadly speaking share an impulse, as Gabriel Pérez-Barreiro has written, "to complicate the discoveries of the 1950s and 60s, the era of heroic modernism, and to update them to very contemporary questions of perception. . . . A revival of formal solutions is not only not desirable but actually impossible in our current state of contemporaneity."[25] While the present exhibition focuses primarily on artists who have returned to this appropriative stance through the neo-conceptual practices of the 1990s and 2000s, another strength of the gift is its representation of key Conceptual practitioners of the 1970s and 1980s—artists such as Luis Camnitzer, Victor Grippo, Alfredo Jaar, Leandro Katz, David Lamelas, and Meireles—as well as the generation that succeeded them, including Jorge Macchi, Leirner, and José Leonilson.

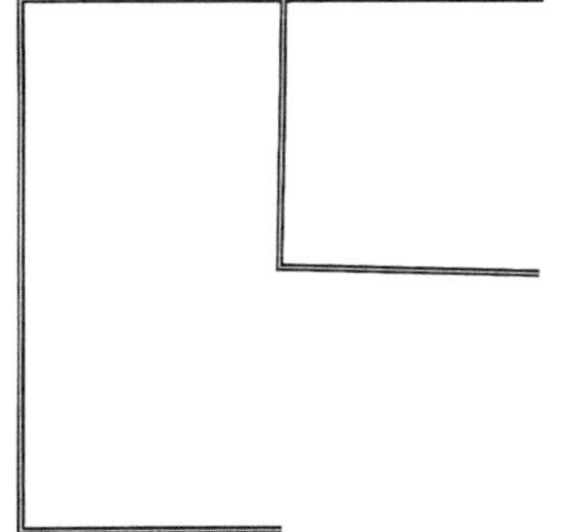

Fig. 9   Waltercio Caldas. *Painted Iron*. 1978. Painted iron, 47 ¼ × 47 ¼ × ⁹⁄₁₆" (120 × 120 × 1.5 cm)

23   Pérez-Oramas, *Arte contemporáneo venezolano en la Colección Cisneros*, 24.

24   In a conversation with Ariel Jiménez, Caldas discusses Velázquez's play with space and perspective in the painting *Cristo en la casa de Marta y María* (1618). See *Waltercio Caldas in Conversation with Ariel Jiménez* (New York: Fundación Cisneros/Colección Patricia Phelps de Cisneros, 2016), 82.

25   Gabriel Pérez-Barreiro, "Foreword," in *Waltercio Caldas: O ar mais próximo e outras matérias*, ed. Adriana Boff (Porto Alegre, Brazil: Fundação Iberê Camargo, 2012), 172.

In 2008, Cisneros's daughter Adriana Cisneros de Griffin became president of the Colección Cisneros and, with Pérez-Barreiro, took an interest in strengthening the contemporary program. Having studied art history at Columbia University at a time when globalization had begun absorbing the historical specificities of regional modernisms into the diffuse geography of the contemporary, Adriana presided over a shift, brought about, in part, by the success of the collection's program.[26] The headquarters were moved from Caracas to New York, and acquisitions over the next few years included works by Suwon Lee, Elena Damiani, Alejandro Cesarco, and Mario García Torres. At the time, Pérez-Barreiro remembers, the market for Latin American art was booming, and collecting priorities shifted to privilege artists from countries with less-developed arts infrastructure and artists without a gallery, for whom the collection would be their first important sale: "We wanted to be at the beginning of the chain," he says, "with the artists in their studios. That made us very different at the time. I thought that if we had the structure that we had, and especially the freedom of thought and action that Patty and Adriana promoted, it would be absurd to do what the others did, and not actively create a differentiated vision for the CPPC. I think we got it."[27] Under Pérez-Barreiro, Cisneros's vision of inserting art from Latin America into more international contexts aligned with a broader profile within increasingly global circuits of visibility. This has become a mission of the collection in and of itself, one that co-directors Ileen Kohn and Alexa Halaby continue to carry out.

In 2011, Pérez-Barreiro hired curator Sofía Hernández Chong Cuy, who had previously served as director of the Museo Tamayo, to focus on contemporary acquisitions. In addition to steering the collection's grant and residency partnerships, she maintained its ties to Venezuela through field research and public programs. The Seminario Fundación Cisneros, originally designed by Jiménez to promote the study of other forms of culture alongside modern and contemporary art, was convened in Caracas by Hernández Chong Cuy from 2012 to 2017.[28] In New York, she expanded the collection's programs to highlight contemporary acquisitions.[29] The series *Viewing Room*, organized with the artist Alejandro Cesarco, presented a single artwork, accompanied by a public program, at changing venues around the city. These programs introduced local audiences to newly acquired works such as Katz's Catherwood Project (plates 2–8, 12–14), Michael Stevenson's *Fountain of Prosperity* (plate 28), and Regina José Galindo's *Looting* (plate 26), some of which had never been exhibited in New York.

26   She told Jiménez, "I am perhaps the first in the family to be directly affected by this project, and for this reason I could say that its objectives were fulfilled in me. I don't feel the need to think in regional terms. I am not interested in Latin American art, or not only. I'm interested in art, period." Ariel Jiménez and Virginia Pérez-Ratton, *Ecos y contrastes: arte contemporáneo en la Colección Cisneros* (Venezuela: Colección Cisneros, 2005), 15.

27   Gabriel Pérez-Barreiro, email message to the author, June 24, 2022.

28   The Seminario Fundación Cisneros joined other public programs, such as *Discusiones* and *Conexiones Emergentes*, initiated by the CPPC to support multidisciplinary exchange and to connect artists, curators, and critics in Venezuela.

29   Among the CPPC programs that Hernández Chong Cuy restructured were residency and grant partnerships with the Skowhegan School of Painting and Sculpture, the Centro Cultural Eduardo León Jimenes, the Center for Curatorial Studies at Bard College, and the International Committee for Museums and Collections of Modern Art.

If Herkenhoff and Pérez-Oramas had conceived of contemporary works by Obregón or Caldas as engaging with the legacies of the modern and traveler artist collections, Pérez-Barreiro and Hernández Chong Cuy developed continuities with the other collecting areas.[30] As Hernández Chong Cuy wrote in 2019:

> The concerns of each of these four other areas find renewed expressions in contemporary artistic practice. From the collection of modernist art, specializing in geometric abstraction, there is an impetus to experiment with forms of artmaking in a perceptual and rational idiom; within the colonial period, there is an emphasis on the sacred and secular uses of art; from the collection of traveler art, there is a focus on the artist as an explorer dedicated to the task of field research and the registration of landscape; and from the Orinoco collection, the consideration of the foundational role of everyday and ceremonial materials in both anthropology and aesthetics.[31]

During Hernández Chong Cuy's tenure, works by Katz, Stevenson, and Galindo, among others, were acquired to resonate with the traveler artists collection. "For example, Katz's work involved revisiting the sites in Yucatán and Central America traveled by Frederick Catherwood during the nineteenth century," she said. "The CPPC acquired both Katz's [The Catherwood Project] and Catherwood's work [*Incidents of Travel in Central America, Chiapas, and Yucatan*, p. 18, fig. 3] the same year."[32] These relationships emerge consistently and resoundingly throughout the Contemporary Gift: works by José Alejandro Restrepo (plate 16), Lothar Baumgarten (fig. 10), and Katz respond to depictions of the Latin American landscape seen through foreign eyes, while an engagement with alternate histories of modernism (as Katzenstein details elsewhere in this catalogue) inform the methods of Armando Andrade Tudela, Cildo Meireles, Mauro Restiffe, and Mario García Torres.

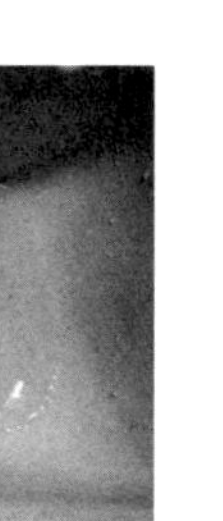

Fig. 10   Lothar Baumgarten. *A Voyage, or 'With the MS Remscheid on the Amazon' or the Account of a Voyage under the Stars of the Refrigerator*. 1968–71. Eighty-one 35mm black-and-white and color slides, 13 min. loop

At MoMA, Pérez-Oramas became the Estrellita Brodsky Curator of Latin American Art in 2006. An important opportunity for revision of the Museum's collection came through the exhibition *MoMA at El Museo: Latin American and Caribbean Art from the Collection of The Museum of Modern Art* (2004), a curatorial collaboration between MoMA and El Museo del Barrio.[33] The exhibition brought Orozco's *The Subway* and Rivera's *May Day, Moscow* into dialogue with Cisneros's gifts of Meireles's *Thread* (plate 55) and works by Lygia Pape and Hélio Oiticica,

30   Pérez-Barreiro remembers that Herkenhoff's interest in the connections between traveler artists and contemporary art resulted in acquisitions of works by Franz Ackerman, Andreas Gursky, and others. Jiménez's essays for early CPPC exhibitions in Chile, Peru, and Mexico also demonstrate that these ongoing dialogues have been central to the collection's identity. In 2017, the CPPC collaborated with the Olana Partnership on the exhibition *OVERLOOK: Teresita Fernández Confronts Frederic Church at Olana*, in which Fernández responded to Frederic Church and traveler artists in a site-specific installation at Church's historic home in Hudson, New York.

31   Sofía Hernández Chong Cuy, *Portadores de sentido: Arte contemporáneo en la Colección Patricia Phelps de Cisneros* (New York: Colección Patricia Phelps de Cisneros, 2019), 116.

32   Sofía Hernández Chong Cuy, interview with the author, August 11, 2022.

33   Smaller-scale opportunities to present the Latin American collection in integrated ways include Paulo Herkenhoff's exhibitions *The Marriage of Reason and Squalor* (2000) and *Tempo* (2002).

as well as highlighting the Museum's most recent acquisitions of Doris Salcedo, Guillermo Kuitca, Gabriel Orozco, and others. In 2009, the International Program, directed by Jay Levenson, developed the internal research and curatorial initiative Contemporary and Modern Art Perspectives (C-MAP). Originally organized into regional groups focused on modern and contemporary art produced in Asia, Central and Eastern Europe, Latin America, and, later, Africa, the program encourages cross-departmental collaboration and axes of transnational thinking that reflect many of the goals of the Colección Cisneros. C-MAP research has resulted in innovative exhibitions such as *Transmissions: Art in Eastern Europe and Latin America, 1960–1980* (2015–16) and *Fotoclubismo: Brazilian Modernist Photography, 1946–1964* (2021, fig. 11). As part of *Transmissions*, Lamelas periodically staged, with members of the public, his performance-based work *Time* (1970) (plate 68). In 2020, C-MAP Latin America merged its program into the newly established Cisneros Research Institute for the Study of Art from Latin America.

Fig. 11   Exhibition catalogue for *Fotoclubismo: Brazilian Modernist Photography and the Foto-Cine Clube Bandeirante, 1946–1964* , edited by Sarah Hermanson Meister (New York: The Museum of Modern Art, 2021)

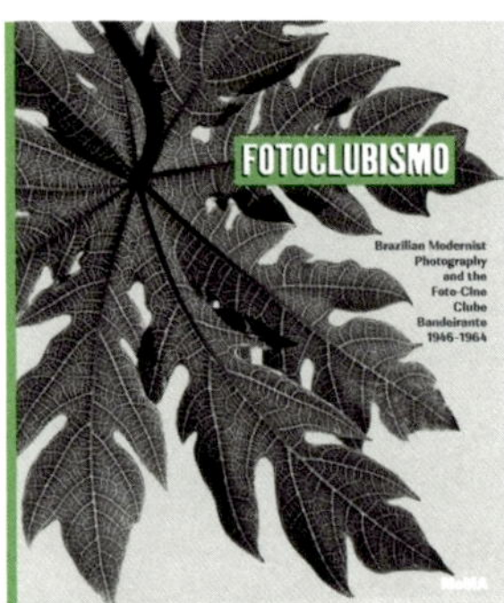

While Pérez-Oramas and Elderfield had conceived of the Cisneros Modern and Contemporary Gifts as a unified whole, in conversation with Lowry they decided that the two would be given separately. In January 2018 the Colección Cisneros completed the gift with ninety works of contemporary art by forty-eight artists representing ten Latin American countries, significantly enhancing the Museum's holdings of works from the region. After Pérez-Oramas's departure, Stuart Comer, Chief Curator of Media and Performance, shepherded the gift to the Museum's curatorial departments in collaboration with Levenson. Like the Modern Gift, defined by its transnational focus on geometric abstraction, the contemporary works reflect a global view, this time marked by a shift toward video, performance, photography, and more participatory forms of art. At the same time, they establish an important dialogue between an emerging generation of artists and the Museum's historical holdings of photography, media and performance, and Conceptual art. As with the Modern Gift, the Contemporary Gift demonstrates the globalization of many of these practices, enabling MoMA to present a story, through its collection, that is ever more nuanced and inclusive.

Armando Andrade Tudela (Peruvian, born 1975)
Camión (*Truck*)
2003
Sixty 35mm color slides
5 min. loop
The Museum of Modern Art, New York. Latin American and Caribbean Fund through gift of Adriana Cisneros de Griffin and Ernesto Poma

Armando Andrade Tudela (Peruvian, born 1975)
Huaco deforme (*Deformed Pottery*)
2012
16mm film transferred to video (color, silent)
2:12 min.
The Museum of Modern Art, New York. Gift of Patricia Phelps de Cisneros through the Latin American and Caribbean Fund in honor of Carlos Rodríguez-Pastor

Firelei Báez (Dominican, born 1981)
Untitled (Terra Nova)
2020
Oil and acrylic paint, laser print on canvas
102 13⁄16 × 132 5⁄16 × 1 9⁄16" (261.1 × 336.1 × 4 cm)
Montreal Museum of Fine Arts, Purchase, W. Bruce C. Bailey Fête-champêtre Fund, Douglas Bensadoun Fund, Diana Billes Fund and Fund of the Women of Influence Circle

Laura Anderson Barbata (Mexican, born 1958)
Autorretrato (*Self-Portrait*), from Intercambios, Amazonas Venezuela (Exchanges, Amazonas Venezuela)
1996–98
Silver dye bleach print
16 × 13" (40.6 × 33 cm)
Colección Patricia Phelps de Cisneros

Laura Anderson Barbata (Mexican, born 1958)
Conejo, from Intercambios, Amazonas Venezuela (Exchanges, Amazonas Venezuela)
1996–98
Silver dye bleach print
13 × 16" (33 × 40.6 cm)
Colección Patricia Phelps de Cisneros

Laura Anderson Barbata (Mexican, born 1958)
En el orden del caos (*In the Order of Chaos*), from Intercambios, Amazonas Venezuela (Exchanges, Amazonas Venezuela)
1996–98
Silver dye bleach print
13 × 16" (33 × 40.6 cm)
Colección Patricia Phelps de Cisneros

Laura Anderson Barbata (Mexican, born 1958)
Rober, from Intercambios, Amazonas Venezuela (Exchanges, Amazonas Venezuela)
1996–98
Silver dye bleach print
16 × 13" (40.6 × 33 cm)
Colección Patricia Phelps de Cisneros

José Bedia (Cuban, born 1959)
Mamá Kalunga
1992
Acrylic and wood on canvas
66 15⁄16 × 118 1⁄8 × 4" (170 × 300 × 10.2 cm)
Colección Patricia Phelps de Cisneros

Alejandro Cesarco (Uruguayan, born 1975)
Present Memory
2009
Video (color, silent)
3 min.
The Museum of Modern Art, New York. Gift of Patricia Phelps de Cisneros through the Latin American and Caribbean Fund

Alejandro Cesarco (Uruguayan, born 1975)
Studies for a Series on Love (Wendy's Hands)
2015
Two archival inkjet prints, framed
Each: 10 7⁄16 × 12 3⁄16" (26.5 × 31 cm)
Collection the artist

Elena Damiani (Peruvian, born 1979)
Fading Field No. 1
2012
Inkjet print on silk chiffon with wooden frame and black wall
69 3⁄4 × 52 7⁄8" (177.2 × 134.3 cm)
The Museum of Modern Art, New York. Gift of Patricia Phelps de Cisneros through the Latin American and Caribbean Fund in honor of Mimi Haas

Iran do Espírito Santo (Brazilian, born 1963)
En Passant 10
2023
Site-specific wall painting
Collection the artist

Regina José Galindo (Guatemalan, born 1974)
Looting
2010
Eight gold fillings
Dimensions variable
The Museum of Modern Art, New York. Gift of Patricia Phelps de Cisneros through the Latin American and Caribbean Fund

Sofía Gallisá Muriente (Puerto Rican, born 1986)
Asimilar y destruir (*Assimilate and Destroy*)
2019
16mm film transferred to video (black and white, silent)
2:38 min.
The Museum of Modern Art, New York. Fund for the Twenty-First Century

Mario García Torres (Mexican, born 1975)
Je ne sais si c'en est la cause
2009
Fifty-eight 35mm color slides and two vinyl LPs
11:50 min.
The Museum of Modern Art, New York. Gift of Patricia Phelps de Cisneros through the Latin American and Caribbean Fund in honor of Sofía Hernández Chong Cuy

Sheroanawë Hakihiiwë (Venezuelan and Yanomami, born 1971)
Masiko (*Shelter*)
2018
Acrylic on paper
19 ¾ × 27 ⁹⁄₁₆" (50.2 × 70 cm)
The Museum of Modern Art, New York. Latin American and Caribbean Fund

Sheroanawë Hakihiiwë (Venezuelan and Yanomami, born 1971)
Hereremi kaweiki (*Beard of an Insect*)
2019
Ink on paper
19 ¾ × 27 ½" (50.2 × 69.9 cm)
The Museum of Modern Art, New York. Latin American and Caribbean Fund

Sheroanawë Hakihiiwë (Venezuelan and Yanomami, born 1971)
Hii Hipe raharaki (*Small Branches*)
2020
Ink on paper
29 ¾ × 18 ⅞" (75.6 × 48 cm)
The Museum of Modern Art, New York. Latin American and Caribbean Fund

Sheroanawë Hakihiiwë (Venezuelan and Yanomami, born 1971)
Shihitima thothope (*Stinging Vine*)
2020
Acrylic on colored paper
19 ⅞ × 26 ¾" (50.5 × 68 cm)
The Museum of Modern Art, New York. Gift of Adriana Cisneros de Griffin in honor of Patricia Phelps de Cisneros through the Latin American and Caribbean Fund

Sheroanawë Hakihiiwë (Venezuelan and Yanomami, born 1971)
Aro Koshi (*Wild Fruits*)
2021
Acrylic on colored paper
37 × 25" (94 × 63.5 cm)
The Museum of Modern Art, New York. Latin American and Caribbean Fund

Sheroanawë Hakihiiwë (Venezuelan and Yanomami, born 1971)
Pohoroa ana si (*Cacao*)
2021
Acrylic on colored paper
37 × 25" (94 × 63.5 cm)
The Museum of Modern Art, New York. Latin American and Caribbean Fund

Sheroanawë Hakihiiwë (Venezuelan and Yanomami, born 1971)
Sitio Siki (*Bromeliads*)
2021
Acrylic on colored paper
37 × 25" (94 × 63.5 cm)
The Museum of Modern Art, New York. Gift of Patricia Phelps de Cisneros in honor of Adriana Cisneros de Griffin through the Latin American and Caribbean Fund

Sheroanawë Hakihiiwë (Venezuelan and Yanomami, born 1971)
Wapu (*Fruits*)
2021
Acrylic on colored paper
37 × 25" (94 × 63.5 cm)
The Museum of Modern Art, New York. Latin American and Caribbean Fund

Leandro Katz (Argentine, born 1938)
El Castillo (Chichén Itzá) (*The Castle [Chichén Itzá]*), from The Catherwood Project
1985
Gelatin silver print
20 × 16" (50.8 × 40.6 cm)
The Museum of Modern Art, New York. Promised gift of Patricia Phelps de Cisneros through the Latin American and Caribbean Fund in honor of May Castleberry

Leandro Katz (Argentine, born 1938)
Kabah, a la manera de Catherwood (Templo de las Máscaras) (*Kabah, after Catherwood [Temple of the Masks]*), from The Catherwood Project
1985
Gelatin silver print
16 × 20" (40.6 × 50.8 cm)
The Museum of Modern Art, New York. Promised gift of Patricia Phelps de Cisneros through the Latin American and Caribbean Fund in honor of May Castleberry

Leandro Katz (Argentine, born 1938)
Tulúm, a la manera de Catherwood (El Castillo) (*Tulúm, after Catherwood [The Castle]*), from The Catherwood Project
1985
Gelatin silver print
16 × 20" (40.6 × 50.8 cm)
The Museum of Modern Art, New York. Promised gift of Patricia Phelps de Cisneros through the Latin American and Caribbean Fund in honor of May Castleberry

Leandro Katz (Argentine, born 1938)
Uxmal, a la manera de Catherwood (Casa de la Monjas, esq. sureste) (*Uxmal, after Catherwood [House of the Nuns, Southeast Corner]*), from The Catherwood Project
1985
Gelatin silver print
16 × 20" (40.6 × 50.8 cm)
The Museum of Modern Art, New York. Promised gift of Patricia Phelps de Cisneros through the Latin American and Caribbean Fund in honor of May Castleberry

Leandro Katz (Argentine, born 1938)
Templo de la Frondosa Cruz, Palenque (*Temple of the Foliated Cross, Palenque*), from The Catherwood Project
1986
Gelatin silver print
16 × 20" (40.6 × 50.8 cm)
The Museum of Modern Art, New York. Promised gift of Patricia Phelps de Cisneros through the Latin American and Caribbean Fund in honor of May Castleberry

Leandro Katz (Argentine, born 1938)
Ídolo a medio enterrar, Copán (*Half-Buried Idol, Copán*), from The Catherwood Project
1989
Gelatin silver print
20 × 16" (50.8 × 40.6 cm)
The Museum of Modern Art, New York. Promised gift of Patricia Phelps de Cisneros through the Latin American and Caribbean Fund in honor of May Castleberry

Leandro Katz (Argentine, born 1938)
Arco de Labná, a la manera de Catherwood (fachada del este) (*Labná's Arch, after Catherwood [East Facade]*), from The Catherwood Project
1991
Gelatin silver print
20 × 16" (50.8 × 40.6 cm)
The Museum of Modern Art, New York. Promised gift of Patricia Phelps de Cisneros through the Latin American and Caribbean Fund in honor of May Castleberry

Leandro Katz (Argentine, born 1938)
Arco de Labná, Interior, a la manera de Catherwood (*Labná's Arch, Interior, after Catherwood*), from The Catherwood Project
1991
Gelatin silver print
20 × 16" (50.8 × 40.6 cm)
The Museum of Modern Art, New York. Promised gift of Patricia Phelps de Cisneros through the Latin American and Caribbean Fund in honor of May Castleberry

Leandro Katz (Argentine, born 1938)
Kabah, Interior, a la manera de Catherwood (*Kabah, Interior [After Catherwood]*), from The Catherwood Project
1993
Gelatin silver print
20 × 16" (50.8 × 40.6 cm)
The Museum of Modern Art, New York. Promised gift of Patricia Phelps de Cisneros through the Latin American and Caribbean Fund in honor of May Castleberry

Leandro Katz (Argentine, born 1938)
Uxmal, Casa de las Palomas (*Uxmal, House of the Doves*), from The Catherwood Project
1993
Gelatin silver print
16 × 20" (40.6 × 50.8 cm)
The Museum of Modern Art, New York. Promised gift of Patricia Phelps de Cisneros through the Latin American and Caribbean Fund in honor of May Castleberry

Gabriel Kuri (Mexican, born 1970)
Sin título (Superama II) (*Untitled [Superama II]*)
2005
Wool
44 ½ × 91 ⁵⁄₁₆" (113 × 232 cm)
The Museum of Modern Art, New York. Gift of Patricia Phelps de Cisneros through the Latin American and Caribbean Fund in honor of Ramiro Ortiz Mayorga

Maria Laet (Brazilian, born 1982)
Notas sobre o limite do mar (*Notes on the Limit of the Sea*)
2011
Video (color, silent)
11:42 min.
The Museum of Modern Art, New York. Gift of Patricia Phelps de Cisneros through the Latin American and Caribbean Fund in honor of Adriana Catalina Santiago de Cisneros

David Lamelas (Argentine, born 1946)
Time
1970
Gelatin silver print
9 ¹⁄₁₆ × 22 ⁵⁄₁₆" (23 × 56.7 cm)
The Museum of Modern Art, New York. Gift of Patricia Phelps de Cisneros through the Latin American and Caribbean Fund in honor of Kathy Halbreich

Suwon Lee (Venezuelan, born 1977)
La ciudad más peligrosa del mundo (*The Most Dangerous City in the World*)
2011
Inkjet print
36 ¼ × 47 ⅛" (92.1 × 119.7 cm)
The Museum of Modern Art, New York. Gift of Patricia Phelps de Cisneros through the Latin American and Caribbean Fund

Suwon Lee (Venezuelan, born 1977)
Lights On
2011
Inkjet print
36 ¼ × 47 ¼" (92 × 120 cm)
The Museum of Modern Art, New York. Promised gift of Patricia Phelps de Cisneros through the Latin American and Caribbean Fund in honor of Carolina Cisneros Phelps

Suwon Lee (Venezuelan, born 1977)
Purple Haze
2011
Inkjet print
36 ¼ × 47 ¼" (92 × 120 cm)
The Museum of Modern Art, New York. Gift of Patricia Phelps de Cisneros through the Latin American and Caribbean Fund in honor of Clara Rodríguez-Cisneros

Anna Maria Maiolino (Brazilian, born Italy 1942)
Por um fio (*By a Thread*), from Fotopoemação (Photopoemaction)
1976/2017
Black-and-white inkjet print
20 ½ × 31 ⅛" (52 × 79 cm)
Collection the artist and Hauser & Wirth

Gilda Mantilla (Peruvian, born United States 1967)
Raimond Chaves (Colombian, born 1963)
Secretos de la Amazonía (*Secrets of the Amazon*)
2011
Two sets of forty 35mm black-and-white slides
The Museum of Modern Art, New York. Gift of Patricia Phelps de Cisneros through the Latin American and Caribbean Fund in honor of Juan Carlos Verme

Cildo Meireles (Brazilian, born 1948)
Malhas da liberdade (*Meshes of Freedom*)
1976/1977
Iron and glass
47 ¼ × 48 ¼ × 1 ½" (120 × 122.6 × 3.8 cm)
The Museum of Modern Art, New York. Gift of Patricia Phelps de Cisneros through the Latin American and Caribbean Fund in honor of Paulo Herkenhoff

Cildo Meireles (Brazilian, born 1948)
Fio (*Thread*)
1990–95
Forty-eight bales of hay, one 18-carat gold needle, and 100 meters of gold thread
Approximately 85 × 73 × 72" (215.9 × 185.4 × 182.9 cm)
The Museum of Modern Art, New York. Gift of Patricia Phelps de Cisneros

Luis Molina-Pantin (Venezuelan, born Switzerland 1969)
Mouse Pad, from Nuevos paisajes (New Landscapes)
1999–2000
Silver dye bleach print
53 ⅛ × 64 ¹⁵⁄₁₆" (135 × 165 cm)
The Museum of Modern Art, New York. Gift of Patricia Phelps de Cisneros through the Latin American and Caribbean Fund in honor of Adriana Cisneros de Griffin

Aline Motta (Brazilian, born 1974)
(Outros) Fundamentos (*[Other] Foundations*)
2017–19
Video (color, sound)
15:48 min.
The Museum of Modern Art, New York. Latin American and Caribbean Fund

Paulo Nazareth (Brazilian, born 1977)
Antropologia do negro II (*Black Anthropology II*)
2014
High-definition video (black and white, sound)
7:21 min.
The Museum of Modern Art, New York. Latin American and Caribbean Fund

Las Nietas de Nonó (Afro-Caribbean, est. 2011)
mulowayi iyaye nonó (Puerto Rican, born 1979)
mapenzi chibale nonó (Puerto Rican, born 1982)
FOODTOPIA: Después de todo territorio (*FOODTOPIA: After Every Territory*)
2020
Video (color, sound)
27:54 min.
The Museum of Modern Art, New York. Fund for the Twenty-First Century

Roberto Obregón (Venezuelan, born Colombia. 1946–2003)
ADM
1978–90
Acrylic on paper and canvas
52 ¼ × 37 ¼" (132.7 × 94.6 cm)
The Museum of Modern Art, New York. Gift of Patricia Phelps de Cisneros through the Latin American and Caribbean Fund in honor of María Luisa Ferré Rangel

Claudio Perna (Venezuelan, born Italy. 1938–1997)
Haute Couture
1967–68
Metal stand, garden shears, wire, felt, rubber, and rose
47 ⅛ × 11 ½ × 9 ⅛" (119.5 × 29 × 23 cm)
The Museum of Modern Art, New York. Gift of Patricia Phelps de Cisneros through the Latin American and Caribbean Fund in honor of Luis Enrique Pérez-Oramas

Claudio Perna (Venezuelan, born Italy. 1938–1997)
Untitled
1990
Gelatin silver print
11 ¼ × 11 ¼" (28.5 × 28.5 cm)
The Museum of Modern Art, New York. Gift of Patricia Phelps de Cisneros through the Latin American and Caribbean Fund

Gala Porras-Kim (Colombian-Korean, born 1984)
122 Offerings for the Rain at the Peabody Museum
2021
Graphite and ink on paper
46 ⅞ × 35 ⁷⁄₁₆" (119 × 90 cm)
The Museum of Modern Art, New York. Fund for the Twenty-First Century

Gala Porras-Kim (Colombian-Korean, born 1984)
124 Offerings for the Rain at the Peabody Museum
2021
Graphite and ink on paper
46 ⅞ × 35 ⁷⁄₁₆" (119 × 90 cm)
The Museum of Modern Art, New York. Fund for the Twenty-First Century

Gala Porras-Kim (Colombian-Korean, born 1984)
203 Offerings for the Rain at the Peabody Museum
2021
Graphite and ink on paper
46 ⅞ × 35 ⁷⁄₁₆" (119 × 90 cm)
The Museum of Modern Art, New York. Fund for the Twenty-First Century

Gala Porras-Kim (Colombian-Korean, born 1984)
Mediating with the Rain
2021–ongoing
Ink on paper, three pages
Each: 11 × 8 ½" (27.9 × 21.6 cm)
Collection the artist and Commonwealth and Council

Naufus Ramírez-Figueroa (Guatemalan, born 1978)
Cantos de aves extintas previamente desconocidas por la ciencia pero recuperadas a través de sesiones espiritistas No. 2 (Songs of Extinct Birds That Were Previously Unknown to Science But Have Been Rediscovered through Spiritist Sessions No. 2)
2015
Single-channel MP3 audio file
4:09 min.
Collection the artist and Proyectos Ultravioleta

Rosângela Rennó (Brazilian, born 1962)
Wedding Landscape
1996
Gelatin silver negatives and acrylic
44 ¾ × 58 ½ × ½" (113.7 × 148.6 × 1.3 cm)
The Museum of Modern Art, New York. Gift of Patricia Phelps de Cisneros through the Latin American and Caribbean Fund in honor of Sarah Hermanson Meister

Mauro Restiffe (Brazilian, born 1970)
Empossamento #8 (Inauguration No. 8)
2003
Gelatin silver print
14 ½ × 22" (36.8 × 55.9 cm)
The Museum of Modern Art, New York. Gift of Patricia Phelps de Cisneros through the Latin American and Caribbean Fund in honor of André Aranha Corrêa do Lago

Mauro Restiffe (Brazilian, born 1970)
Empossamento #9 (Inauguration No. 9)
2003
Gelatin silver print
14 ½ × 22" (36.8 × 55.9 cm)
The Museum of Modern Art, New York. Gift of Patricia Phelps de Cisneros through the Latin American and Caribbean Fund in honor of Barry Bergdoll

José Alejandro Restrepo (Colombian, born 1959)
Paso del Quindío I (Quindío Pass I)
1992
Three-channel video (black and white, sound) on seventeen cathode-ray-tube monitors
Dimensions variable; 30 min.
The Museum of Modern Art, New York. Gift of Patricia Phelps de Cisneros through the Latin American and Caribbean Fund

Thiago Rocha Pitta (Brazilian, born 1980)
Herança (Heritage)
2007
16mm film transferred to video (color, sound)
11 min.
The Museum of Modern Art, New York. Gift of Patricia Phelps de Cisneros through the Latin American and Caribbean Fund in honor of Sebastián Cisneros-Santiago

Analia Saban (Argentine, born 1980)
Copper Tapestry (ATI Radeon HD 5970 Graphics Card, AMD, 2009)
2020
Woven copper wire and linen thread
138 ½ × 71 ¼" (351.8 × 181 cm)
The Museum of Modern Art, New York. Latin American and Caribbean Fund

Daniel Steegmann Mangrané (Spanish and Brazilian, born 1977)
^
2013
35mm color slide, slide projection equipment, and gold leaf
Installation: 65 × 36 × 55" (165.1 × 91.4 × 139.7 cm)
Collection of Adriana Cisneros de Griffin

Michael Stevenson (New Zealander, born 1964)
The Fountain of Prosperity (Answers to Some Questions about Bananas)
2006
Plexiglass, steel, brass, aluminum, rubber, cork, string, concrete, dyed water, pumps, and fluorescent lamps
96 ⁷⁄₁₆ × 62 ¹³⁄₁₆ × 43 ¹¹⁄₁₆" (245 × 157 × 111 cm)
The Museum of Modern Art, New York. Gift of Patricia Phelps de Cisneros through the Latin American and Caribbean Fund in honor of Gonzalo Parodi

Adrián Villar Rojas (Argentine, born 1980)
Untitled, from the series Los Teatros de Saturno (The Theaters of Saturn)
2014
Iron, gesso, and clay
34 ⁷⁄₁₆ × 61 ¹³⁄₁₆ × 46 ⁷⁄₁₆" (87.5 × 157 × 118 cm)
Colección Patricia Phelps de Cisneros

Las Yeguas del Apocalipsis (Chilean, 1987–1997)
Pedro Mardones Lemebel (Chilean, 1952–2015)
Francisco Casas Silva (Chilean, born 1959)
Las dos Fridas (The Two Fridas)
1989
Inkjet print
49 ³⁄₁₆ × 47 ¼" (125 × 120 cm)
The Museum of Modern Art, New York. Gift of Pedro Montes through the Latin American and Caribbean Fund in honor of Pedro Lemebel and Francisco Casas

All works are gifts or promised gifts to The Museum of Modern Art, New York.

Carlos Amorales (Mexican, born 1970)
Manimal
2005
Video (black and white, sound)
5:30 min.
Gift of Patricia Phelps de Cisneros through the Latin American and Caribbean Fund in honor of Santiago Rodríguez-Cisneros

Armando Andrade Tudela (Peruvian, born 1975)
Huaco deforme (Deformed Pottery)
2012
16mm film transferred to video (color, silent)
2:12 min.
Gift of Patricia Phelps de Cisneros through the Latin American and Caribbean Fund in honor of Carlos Rodríguez-Pastor

Armando Andrade Tudela (Peruvian, born 1975)
Foro (Forum)
2013
16mm film transferred to video (color, sound)
10:53 min.
Gift of Patricia Phelps de Cisneros through the Latin American and Caribbean Fund in honor of Marie-Josée Kravis

Lothar Baumgarten (German, 1944–2018)
A Voyage, or 'With the MS Remscheid on the Amazon' or the Account of a Voyage under the Stars of the Refrigerator
1968–71
Eighty-one 35mm black-and-white and color slides
13 min. loop
Gift of Patricia Phelps de Cisneros through the Latin American and Caribbean Fund in honor of Guillermo A. Cisneros Phelps

Feliza Bursztyn (Colombian, 1933–1982)
Untitled, from Las histéricas (The Hysterics)
c. 1967
Stainless steel and motor
17 ¹¹⁄₁₆ × 15 ¾ × 19 ¹¹⁄₁₆" (45 × 40 × 50 cm)
Gift of Patricia Phelps de Cisneros through the Latin American and Caribbean Fund in honor of Carolina Rodríguez-Cisneros

Waltercio Caldas (Brazilian, born 1946)
Painted Iron
1978
Painted iron
47 ¼ × 47 ¼ × ⁹⁄₁₆" (120 × 120 × 1.5 cm)
Gift of Patricia Phelps de Cisneros through the Latin American and Caribbean Fund in honor of Gabriel Pérez-Barreiro

Luis Camnitzer (Uruguayan, born 1937)
Sentence Reflecting the Sentence that States the Reflection
1975
Wood, glass, and brass
13 ⅞ × 9 ¾ × 2" (35.2 × 24.8 × 5.1 cm)
Gift of Patricia Phelps de Cisneros through the Latin American and Caribbean Fund in honor of Pedro Barbosa

Alejandro Cesarco (Uruguayan, born 1975)
Help!
2002
Video (color, sound)
2 min.
Gift of Patricia Phelps de Cisneros through the Latin American and Caribbean Fund in honor of Stuart Comer

Alejandro Cesarco (Uruguayan, born 1975)
Flowers I–X
2003
Ink on paper receipts, documentation of a performance
10 pieces: 14 × 10 ½" (35.6 × 26.7 cm) each
Gift of Patricia Phelps de Cisneros through the Latin American and Caribbean Fund in honor of Agnes Gund

Alejandro Cesarco (Uruguayan, born 1975)
Index (A Novel)
2003
Four pigmented inkjet prints
Each: 40 × 30" (101.6 × 76.2 cm)
Promised gift of Patricia Phelps de Cisneros through the Latin American and Caribbean Fund in honor of Nicholas Griffin

Alejandro Cesarco (Uruguayan, born 1975)
Present Memory
2009
Video (color, silent)
3 min.
Gift of Patricia Phelps de Cisneros through the Latin American and Caribbean Fund

Elena Damiani (Peruvian, born 1979)
Fading Field No. 1
2012
Inkjet print on silk chiffon with wooden frame
and black wall
69 ¾ × 52 ⅞" (177.2 × 134.3 cm)
Gift of Patricia Phelps de Cisneros through the Latin American and Caribbean Fund in honor of Mimi Haas

Juan Manuel Echavarría (Colombian, born 1947)
Bocas de ceniza (*Mouths of Ash*)
2003–04
Video (color, sound)
18:05 min.
Gift of Patricia Phelps de Cisneros through the Latin American and Caribbean Fund in honor of Ambassador William H. and Wendy Luers

Eugenio Espinoza (Venezuelan, born 1950)
Untitled
1971
Acrylic on canvas
47 ¼ × 47 ¼" (120 × 120 cm)
Gift of Patricia Phelps de Cisneros through the Latin American and Caribbean Fund in honor of Luis Enrique Pérez-Oramas

Héctor Fuenmayor (Venezuelan, born 1949)
Citrus 6906
1973/2014
Wall paint and vinyl
Dimensions variable
Gift of Patricia Phelps de Cisneros through the Latin American and Caribbean Fund in honor of Lord and Lady Foster

Regina José Galindo (Guatemalan, born 1974)
America's Family Prison
2008
Video (color, sound)
54:49 min.
Gift of Patricia Phelps de Cisneros through the Latin American and Caribbean Fund in honor of Agnes Gund and The Art for Justice Fund

Regina José Galindo (Guatemalan, born 1974)
Looting
2010
Eight gold fillings
Dimensions variable
Gift of Patricia Phelps de Cisneros through the Latin American and Caribbean Fund

Mario García Torres (Mexican, born 1975)
Je ne sais si c'en est la cause
2009
Fifty-eight 35mm color slides and two vinyl LPs
11:50 min.
Gift of Patricia Phelps de Cisneros through the Latin American and Caribbean Fund in honor of Sofía Hernández Chong Cuy

Mario García Torres (Mexican, born 1975)
Alguna vez has visto la nieve caer? (*Have you ever seen the snow?*)
2010
Eighty-eight 35mm color slides, audio
6 min. loop
Gift of Patricia Phelps de Cisneros through the Latin American and Caribbean Fund in honor of Jill Kraus

Mario García Torres (Mexican, born 1975)
Xoco, the Kid Who Loved Being Bored (cont.)
2012
16mm film (color, silent, 2:15 min.) and three drawings
Sheet, 14 × 10 ⅞16" (35.5 × 26.5 cm); sheet, 12 ⅜ × 10 ⅞16" (31.5 × 26.5 cm); sheet, 34 × 26 ½" (86.4 × 67.3 cm)
Gift of Patricia Phelps de Cisneros through the Latin American and Caribbean Fund in honor of Rodrigo Cisneros-Santiago

Victor Grippo (Argentine, 1936–2002)
Analogía IV (*Analogy IV*)
1972
Wood table, ceramic and plastic dishes, metal and acrylic utensils, cotton and velvet tablecloth, and organic and plastic potatoes
29 ¾ × 37 ⅛ × 23 ⅛" (75.6 × 94.3 × 58.9 cm)
Gift of Patricia Phelps de Cisneros through the Latin American and Caribbean Fund in honor of Glenn D. Lowry

Alfredo Jaar (Chilean, born 1956)
He Ram
1991
Screenprint ink on mirror
96 ⅟16 × 96 ⅟16 × ⅗16" (244 × 244 × 0.5 cm)
Promised gift of Patricia Phelps de Cisneros through the Latin American and Caribbean Fund in honor of Guillermo A. Cisneros Phelps

Leandro Katz (Argentine, born 1938)
El Castillo (Chichén Itzá) (*The Castle [Chichén Itzá]*), from The Catherwood Project
1985
Gelatin silver print
20 × 16" (50.8 × 40.6 cm)
Promised gift of Patricia Phelps de Cisneros through the Latin American and Caribbean Fund in honor of May Castleberry

Leandro Katz (Argentine, born 1938)
Kabah, a la manera de Catherwood (Templo de las Máscaras) (*Kabah, after Catherwood [Temple of the Masks]*), from The Catherwood Project
1985
Gelatin silver print
16 × 20" (40.6 × 50.8 cm)
Promised gift of Patricia Phelps de Cisneros through the Latin American and Caribbean Fund in honor of May Castleberry

Leandro Katz (Argentine, born 1938)
Tulúm, a la manera de Catherwood (El Castillo) (*Tulúm, after Catherwood [The Castle]*), from The Catherwood Project
1985
Gelatin silver print
16 × 20" (40.6 × 50.8 cm)
Promised gift of Patricia Phelps de Cisneros through the Latin American and Caribbean Fund in honor of May Castleberry

Leandro Katz (Argentine, born 1938)
Uxmal, a la manera de Catherwood (Casa de la Monjas, esq. sureste) (*Uxmal, after Catherwood [House of the Nuns, Southeast Corner]*), from The Catherwood Project
1985
Gelatin silver print
16 × 20" (40.6 × 50.8 cm)
Promised gift of Patricia Phelps de Cisneros through the Latin American and Caribbean Fund in honor of May Castleberry

Leandro Katz (Argentine, born 1938)
Templo de la Frondosa Cruz, Palenque
(*Temple of the Foliated Cross, Palenque*),
from The Catherwood Project
1986
Gelatin silver print
16 × 20" (40.6 × 50.8 cm)
Promised gift of Patricia Phelps de Cisneros
through the Latin American and Caribbean
Fund in honor of May Castleberry

Leandro Katz (Argentine, born 1938)
Ídolo a medio enterrar, Copán
(*Half-Buried Idol, Copán*), from The
Catherwood Project
1989
Gelatin silver print
20 × 16" (50.8 × 40.6 cm)
Promised gift of Patricia Phelps de Cisneros
through the Latin American and Caribbean
Fund in honor of May Castleberry

Leandro Katz (Argentine, born 1938)
*Arco de Labná, a la manera de Catherwood
(fachada del este)* (*Labná's Arch, after
Catherwood [East Facade]*), from The
Catherwood Project
1991
Gelatin silver print
20 × 16" (50.8 × 40.6 cm)
Promised gift of Patricia Phelps de Cisneros
through the Latin American and Caribbean
Fund in honor of May Castleberry

Leandro Katz (Argentine, born 1938)
*Arco de Labná, Interior, a la manera de
Catherwood* (*Labná's Arch, Interior, after
Catherwood*), from The Catherwood
Project
1991
Gelatin silver print
20 × 16" (50.8 × 40.6 cm)
Promised gift of Patricia Phelps de Cisneros
through the Latin American and Caribbean
Fund in honor of May Castleberry

Leandro Katz (Argentine, born 1938)
Kabah, Interior, a la manera de Catherwood
(*Kabah, Interior [After Catherwood]*), from
The Catherwood Project
1993
Gelatin silver print
20 × 16" (50.8 × 40.6 cm)
Promised gift of Patricia Phelps de Cisneros
through the Latin American and Caribbean
Fund in honor of May Castleberry

Leandro Katz (Argentine, born 1938)
Uxmal, Casa de las Palomas (*Uxmal, House
of the Doves*), from The Catherwood
Project
1993
Gelatin silver print
16 × 20" (40.6 × 50.8 cm)
Promised gift of Patricia Phelps de Cisneros
through the Latin American and Caribbean
Fund in honor of May Castleberry

Gabriel Kuri (Mexican, born 1970)
Sin título (Superama II) (*Untitled
[Superama II]*)
2005
Wool
44 ½ × 91 ⁵⁄₁₆" (113 × 232 cm)
Gift of Patricia Phelps de Cisneros through
the Latin American and Caribbean Fund
in honor of Ramiro Ortiz Mayorga

Maria Laet (Brazilian, born 1982)
Notas sobre o limite do mar (*Notes on the
Limit of the Sea*)
2011
Video (color, silent)
11:42 min.
Gift of Patricia Phelps de Cisneros through
the Latin American and Caribbean Fund
in honor of Adriana Catalina Santiago de
Cisneros

David Lamelas (Argentine, born 1946)
Time
1970
Performance and gelatin silver print
Duration variable
Image: 9 ¹⁄₁₆ × 22 ⁵⁄₁₆" (23 × 56.7 cm)
Gift of Patricia Phelps de Cisneros through
the Latin American and Caribbean Fund
in honor of Kathy Halbreich

Suwon Lee (Venezuelan, born 1977)
La ciudad más peligrosa del mundo (*The
Most Dangerous City in the World*)
2011
Inkjet print
36 ¼ × 47 ⅛" (92.1 × 119.7 cm)
Gift of Patricia Phelps de Cisneros through
the Latin American and Caribbean Fund

Suwon Lee (Venezuelan, born 1977)
Lights On
2011
Inkjet print
36 ¼ × 47 ¼" (92 × 120 cm)
Promised gift of Patricia Phelps de
Cisneros through the Latin American and
Caribbean Fund in honor of Carolina
Cisneros Phelps

Suwon Lee (Venezuelan, born 1977)
Purple Haze
2011
Inkjet print
36 ¼ × 47 ¼" (92 × 120 cm)
Gift of Patricia Phelps de Cisneros through
the Latin American and Caribbean Fund
in honor of Clara Rodríguez-Cisneros

Jac Leirner (Brazilian, born 1961)
Nice to Meet You
1997
Business cards, plexiglass, and aluminum
2 ³⁄₁₆ × 64" (5.5 × 162.5 cm)
Gift of Patricia Phelps de Cisneros through
the Latin American and Caribbean Fund
in honor of Luis Enrique Pérez-Oramas

José Leonilson (Brazilian, 1957–1993)
The Japanese Woman
1988
Acrylic on canvas
41 ⁵⁄₁₆ × 61" (105 × 155 cm)
Gift of Patricia Phelps de Cisneros through
the Latin American and Caribbean Fund
in honor of Juan Yarur

Jorge Macchi (Argentine, born 1963)
Pentagrama (*Staff*)
1993
Pillow, pillowcase, ropes, springs,
and nails
31 ½ × 47 ¼ × 3 ⅛" (80 × 120 × 8 cm)
Gift of Patricia Phelps de Cisneros through
the Latin American and Caribbean Fund

Jorge Macchi (Argentine, born 1963)
Amsterdam
2002
Cut paper
48 ¾ × 48 ¾ × 1" (123.8 × 123.8 × 2.5 cm)
Gift of Patricia Phelps de Cisneros through
the Latin American and Caribbean Fund
in honor of Eva Luisa Griffin-Cisneros

Pedro Manrique Figueroa (Colombian, born 1934)
Poesía (*Poetry*)
2008
Fifteen 35mm color slides and slide projector in plywood box
70 × 48 × 96" (177.8 × 121.9 × 243.8 cm)
Gift of Patricia Phelps de Cisneros through the Latin American and Caribbean Fund

Gilda Mantilla (Peruvian, born United States 1967)
Raimond Chaves (Colombian, born 1963)
Secretos de la Amazonía (*Secrets of the Amazon*)
2011
Two sets of forty 35mm black-and-white slides
Gift of Patricia Phelps de Cisneros through the Latin American and Caribbean Fund in honor of Juan Carlos Verme

Cinthia Marcelle (Brazilian, born 1974)
Leitmotiv
2011
Video (color, sound)
4:16 min.
Gift of Patricia Phelps de Cisneros through the Latin American and Caribbean Fund in honor of João Carlos de Figueiredo Ferraz

Cildo Meireles (Brazilian, born 1948)
Para ser curvada com os olhos (*To Be Curved with the Eyes*)
1970/1975
Wood box, iron bars, enamel plaque, glass, and graph paper
4 ½ × 19 ½ × 9 ⅞" (11.4 × 49.5 × 25.1 cm)
Gift of Patricia Phelps de Cisneros through the Latin American and Caribbean Fund in honor of Andrea and José Olympio Pereira

Cildo Meireles (Brazilian, born 1948)
A diferença entre o círculo e a bola é o peso (*The Difference between the Circle and the Sphere Is the Weight*)
1976
Paper and paper bags
Overall dimensions approx. 2 ⅜ × 25 × 15" (6 × 63.5 × 38.1 cm)
Gift of Patricia Phelps de Cisneros through the Latin American and Caribbean Fund in honor of Paulo Herkenhoff

Cildo Meireles (Brazilian, born 1948)
Malhas da liberdade (*Meshes of Freedom*)
1976/1977
Iron and glass
47 ¼ × 48 ¼ × 1 ½" (120 × 122.6 × 3.8 cm)
Gift of Patricia Phelps de Cisneros through the Latin American and Caribbean Fund in honor of Paulo Herkenhoff

Ana Maria Millan (Colombian, born 1975)
Eduardo Carvajal (Colombian, born 1949)
La pieza ensayo (*The Rehearsal Piece*)
2008
Three-channel video (color, sound)
2:22 min., 6:02 min., and 5:25 min.
Gift of Patricia Phelps de Cisneros through the Latin American and Caribbean Fund in honor of Sofía Hernández Chong Cuy

Luis Molina-Pantin (Venezuelan, born Switzerland 1969)
Mouse Pad, from Nuevos paisajes (New Landscapes)
1999–2000
Silver dye bleach print
53 ⅛ × 64 ¹⁵⁄₁₆" (135 × 165 cm)
Gift of Patricia Phelps de Cisneros through the Latin American and Caribbean Fund in honor of Adriana Cisneros de Griffin

Juan Nascimento (Venezuelan, born 1969)
Daniela Lovera (Venezuelan, born 1968)
Wuthering Heights
2001
Video (black and white, sound)
3 min.
Gift of Patricia Phelps de Cisneros through the Latin American and Caribbean Fund in honor of Gabriela Rangel

Roberto Obregón (Venezuelan, born Colombia. 1946–2003)
El Agua como un ciclo (*Water as a Cycle*)
1978
Cut and pasted paper and printed paper, watercolor, stamped ink, pencil, paint, typewriting, and glassine envelopes with wax on three sheets of paper with embossing
Each: 30 ½ × 24 ½" (77.5 × 62.2 cm)
Gift of Patricia Phelps de Cisneros through the Latin American and Caribbean Fund in honor of Sharon Schultz

Roberto Obregón (Venezuelan, born Colombia. 1946–2003)
ADM
1978–90
Acrylic on canvas
52 ¼ × 37 ¼" (132.7 × 94.6 cm)
Gift of Patricia Phelps de Cisneros through the Latin American and Caribbean Fund in honor of María Luisa Ferré Rangel

Fernando Ortega (Mexican, born 1971)
Narrow Day
2011
Video (color, sound)
4:54 min.
Gift of Patricia Phelps de Cisneros through the Latin American and Caribbean Fund in honor of Bárbara Garza Lagüera

Bernardo Ortiz Campo (Colombian, born 1972)
Untitled (*Huevo 20 y 21st de oct. 2010*) (*Egg, October 20 and 21st, 2010*)
2010
Enamel on waxed paper
26 × 37" (66 × 94 cm)
Gift of Patricia Phelps de Cisneros through the Latin American and Caribbean Fund in honor of Ellen Susman

Bernardo Ortiz Campo (Colombian, born 1972)
Untitled (*Nunca estoy despierto. 24–26 de sept*) (*I Am Never Awake. September 24–26*)
2010
Enamel and acrylic gel medium on two sheets of waxed paper
Each: 37 × 26" (94 × 66 cm)
Gift of Patricia Phelps de Cisneros through the Latin American and Caribbean Fund in honor of Karen Grimson

César Paternosto (Argentine, born 1931)
The Hidden Order
1972
Acrylic on canvas
42 × 42 × 2 ¾" (106.7 × 106.7 × 7 cm)
Gift of Patricia Phelps de Cisneros through the Latin American and Caribbean Fund in honor of Nando Parrado

Alejandro Paz Navas (Guatemalan,
born 1975)
Guardaespaldas (*The Bodyguard*)
2002
Video (color, sound, 14:30 min.) and six
chromogenic color prints, each: 7 ⅞ ×
9 ¹³⁄₁₆" (20 × 25 cm)
Gift of Patricia Phelps de Cisneros through
the Latin American and Caribbean Fund
in memory of Virginia Pérez-Ratton

Claudio Perna (Venezuelan, born Italy.
1938–1997)
Haute Couture
1967–68
Metal stand, garden shears, wire, felt,
rubber, and rose
47 ⅛ × 11 ½ × 9 ⅛" (119.5 × 29 × 23 cm)
Gift of Patricia Phelps de Cisneros through
the Latin American and Caribbean Fund
in honor of Luis Enrique Pérez-Oramas

Claudio Perna (Venezuelan, born Italy.
1938–1997)
Untitled
c. 1970
Photocopy on paper
8 ½ × 14 ¼" (21.6 × 36.2 cm)
Gift of Patricia Phelps de Cisneros through
the Latin American and Caribbean Fund
in honor of Federica Rodríguez-Cisneros

Claudio Perna (Venezuelan, born Italy.
1938–1997)
Pirámide (*Pyramid*)
c. 1974
Gelatin silver print, pencil and ink on
paper
7 ½ × 9 ⅝" (19 × 24.5 cm)
Gift of Patricia Phelps de Cisneros through
the Latin American and Caribbean Fund

Claudio Perna (Venezuelan, born Italy.
1938–1997)
Deformed Figures Series
c. 1975
Ten color Polaroids
Overall 16 ⁹⁄₁₆ × 28 ¾" (42 × 73 cm)
Gift of Patricia Phelps de Cisneros through
the Latin American and Caribbean Fund

Claudio Perna (Venezuelan, born Italy.
1938–1997)
Aerial View of Caracas
c. 1980
Offset lithograph with gelatin silver print
and felt-tipped pen
24 ½ × 33 ½" (62.2 × 85.1 cm)
Gift of Patricia Phelps de Cisneros through
the Latin American and Caribbean Fund
in honor of Rafael Romero

Claudio Perna (Venezuelan, born Italy.
1938–1997)
Untitled
c. 1980–96
Gelatin silver print
11 ⁷⁄₁₆ × 11 ¼" (29 × 28.5 cm)
Gift of Patricia Phelps de Cisneros through
the Latin American and Caribbean Fund

Claudio Perna (Venezuelan, born Italy.
1938–1997)
Untitled
c. 1980–96
Gelatin silver print
11 ¼ × 11 ¼" (28.5 × 28.5 cm)
Gift of Patricia Phelps de Cisneros through
the Latin American and Caribbean Fund

Claudio Perna (Venezuelan, born Italy.
1938–1997)
Untitled
c. 1980–96
Gelatin silver print
11 ¼ × 11 ¼" (28.5 × 28.5 cm)
Gift of Patricia Phelps de Cisneros through
the Latin American and Caribbean Fund

Claudio Perna (Venezuelan, born Italy.
1938–1997)
Untitled
c. 1980–96
Gelatin silver print
11 ¼ × 11 ¼" (28.5 × 28.5 cm)
Gift of Patricia Phelps de Cisneros through
the Latin American and Caribbean Fund
in honor of Catalina Cisneros-Santiago

Claudio Perna (Venezuelan, born Italy.
1938–1997)
Untitled
c. 1980–96
Gelatin silver print
11 ¼ × 11 ¼" (28.5 × 28.5 cm)
Gift of Patricia Phelps de Cisneros through
the Latin American and Caribbean Fund

Claudio Perna (Venezuelan, born Italy.
1938–1997)
Untitled
c. 1980–96
Gelatin silver print
11 ¼ × 11 ¼" (28.5 × 28.5 cm)
Gift of Patricia Phelps de Cisneros through
the Latin American and Caribbean Fund

Claudio Perna (Venezuelan, born Italy.
1938–1997)
Untitled
c. 1980–96
Gelatin silver print
11 ¼ × 11 ¼" (28.5 × 28.5 cm)
Gift of Patricia Phelps de Cisneros through
the Latin American and Caribbean Fund

Claudio Perna (Venezuelan, born Italy.
1938–1997)
Untitled
c. 1980–96
Gelatin silver print
11 ¼ × 11 ¼" (28.5 × 28.5 cm)
Gift of Patricia Phelps de Cisneros through
the Latin American and Caribbean Fund in
honor of Tomás Orinoco Griffin-Cisneros

Claudio Perna (Venezuelan, born Italy.
1938–1997)
Aerial View of Maracaibo
c. 1985
Gelatin silver print with offset lithograph
30 ⁵⁄₁₆ × 30 ⁵⁄₁₆" (77 × 77 cm)
Gift of Patricia Phelps de Cisneros through
the Latin American and Caribbean Fund
in honor of Samuel Guillén

Amalia Pica (Argentine, born 1978)
Stage (as seen on Afghan Star)
2011
Cardboard, wood, tape, and spotlight
10 × 110 × 110" (25.4 × 279.4 × 279.4 cm)
Gift of Patricia Phelps de Cisneros through
the Latin American and Caribbean Fund
in honor of Anna Deavere Smith

Amalia Pica (Argentine, born 1978)
Venn Diagrams (Under the Spotlight)
2011
Spotlights and motion sensors
Dimensions variable
Gift of Patricia Phelps de Cisneros through
the Latin American and Caribbean Fund
in honor of Stuart Comer

Wilfredo Prieto (Cuban, born 1978)
Mute
2006
Light installation
Dimensions variable
Gift of Patricia Phelps de Cisneros through the Latin American and Caribbean Fund in honor of Gustavo Rodríguez-Cisneros

Rosângela Rennó (Brazilian, born 1962)
Wedding Landscape
1996
Gelatin silver negatives and acrylic
44 ¾ × 58 ½ × ½" (113.7 × 148.6 × 1.3 cm)
Gift of Patricia Phelps de Cisneros through the Latin American and Caribbean Fund in honor of Sarah Hermanson Meister

José Resende (Brazilian, born 1945)
Untitled
1974
Copper, aluminum, and stones
94 ½ × 90 ⁹⁄₁₆ × 23 ⅝" (240 × 230 × 60 cm)
Gift of Patricia Phelps de Cisneros through the Latin American and Caribbean Fund in honor of Todd Bishop

Mauro Restiffe (Brazilian, born 1970)
Empossamento #8 (Inauguration No. 8)
2003
Gelatin silver print
14 ½ × 22" (36.8 × 55.9 cm)
Gift of Patricia Phelps de Cisneros through the Latin American and Caribbean Fund in honor of André Aranha Corrêa do Lago

Mauro Restiffe (Brazilian, born 1970)
Empossamento #9 (Inauguration No. 9)
2003
Gelatin silver print
14 ½ × 22" (36.8 × 55.9 cm)
Gift of Patricia Phelps de Cisneros through the Latin American and Caribbean Fund in honor of Barry Bergdoll

José Alejandro Restrepo (Colombian, born 1959)
Paso del Quindío I (Quindío Pass I)
1992
Three-channel video (black and white, sound) on seventeen cathode-ray-tube monitors
Dimensions variable; 30 min.
Gift of Patricia Phelps de Cisneros through the Latin American and Caribbean Fund

Miguel Rio Branco (Brazilian, born 1946)
Blue Tango
1984
Twenty silver dye bleach prints
Overall 51 ¾ × 62 ³⁄₁₆" (131.4 × 158 cm)
Gift of Patricia Phelps de Cisneros through the Latin American and Caribbean Fund in honor of Adriana Cisneros de Griffin

Thiago Rocha Pitta (Brazilian, born 1980)
Herança (Heritage)
2007
16mm film transferred to video (color, sound)
11 min.
Gift of Patricia Phelps de Cisneros through the Latin American and Caribbean Fund in honor of Sebastián Cisneros-Santiago

Michael Stevenson (New Zealander, born 1964)
The Fountain of Prosperity (Answers to Some Questions about Bananas)
2006
Plexiglass, steel, brass, aluminum, rubber, cork, string, concrete, dyed water, pumps, and fluorescent lamps
96 ⁷⁄₁₆ × 61 ¹³⁄₁₆ × 43 ¹¹⁄₁₆" (245 × 157 × 111 cm)
Gift of Patricia Phelps de Cisneros through the Latin American and Caribbean Fund in honor of Gonzalo Parodi

José Antonio Suárez Londoño (Colombian, born 1955)
Metamorfosis Ovidio I (Metamorphoses Ovid I)
2003
Notebook with pencil, ink, paint, and thread on paper
6 ¾ × 9 × 1" (17.1 × 22.9 × 2.5 cm)
Gift of Patricia Phelps de Cisneros through the Latin American and Caribbean Fund in honor of Luis Enrique Pérez-Oramas

José Antonio Suárez Londoño (Colombian, born 1955)
Metamorfosis Ovidio II (Metamorphoses Ovid II)
2003
Notebook with pencil, ink, paint, and thread on paper
6 ¾ × 9 × 1" (17.1 × 22.9 × 2.5 cm)
Gift of Patricia Phelps de Cisneros through the Latin American and Caribbean Fund in honor of Luis Enrique Pérez-Oramas

José Antonio Suárez Londoño (Colombian, born 1955)
Metamorfosis Ovidio III (Metamorphoses Ovid III)
2003
Notebook with pencil, ink, paint, and thread on paper
6 ¾ × 9 × 1" (17.1 × 22.9 × 2.5 cm)
Gift of Patricia Phelps de Cisneros through the Latin American and Caribbean Fund in honor of Luis Enrique Pérez-Oramas

Yeni & Nan (Venezuelan, est. 1977)
Nan González (Venezuelan, born 1956)
Jennifer Hackshaw (Venezuelan, born 1948)
Autólogica: Agua + Aire (Autologous between Water and Air)
1981
Thirty-two color instant prints (Polaroids)
Overall approx. 48 ⅜ × 10 ½" (122.9 × 26.7 cm)
Gift of Patricia Phelps de Cisneros through the Latin American and Caribbean Fund

Yeni & Nan (Venezuelan, est. 1977)
Nan González (Venezuelan, born 1956)
Jennifer Hackshaw (Venezuelan, born 1948)
Integraciones en agua (Integrations in Water)
1981
Forty-eight color instant prints (Polaroids)
Overall 11 × 55 ⁹⁄₁₆" (28 × 141.2 cm)
Gift of Patricia Phelps de Cisneros through the Latin American and Caribbean Fund in honor of Mauro Herlitzka

David Zink Yi (Peruvian, born 1973)
Untitled
2014
Gelatin silver print
23 ⁹⁄₁₆ × 29 ¹³⁄₁₆" (59.8 × 75.8 cm)
Gift of Patricia Phelps de Cisneros through the Latin American and Caribbean Fund in honor of Eduardo Hochschild

David Zink Yi (Peruvian, born 1973)
Untitled
2014
Gelatin silver print
23 ⁹⁄₁₆ × 29 ¹³⁄₁₆" (59.8 × 75.8 cm)
Gift of Patricia Phelps de Cisneros through the Latin American and Caribbean Fund in honor of Eduardo Hochschild

All works © 2023 the artist unless otherwise noted. Certain credits appear at the request of the artist or artist's representatives. In reproducing the images contained in this publication, The Museum of Modern Art has obtained the permissions of the rights holders wherever possible. Should the Museum have been unable to locate a rights holder, notwithstanding good-faith efforts, it requests that any contact information concerning such rights holders be forwarded, so that they may be contacted for future editions.

Archivo Fundación Museo Amano, © Mika Amano: 62; © Laura Anderson Barbata: back cover (center left), 72; © Estate of Lothar Baumgarten: 107; © José Bedia, courtesy the artist and Fredric Snitzer Gallery: 74; © Armando Andrade Tudela: 68, 75; © Firelei Báez: 38; © Waltercio Caldas: 105; © Alejandro Cesarco, images courtesy the artist: back cover (far right), 84, 87, 96; Colección Eduardo Salazar Yusti, photo Oscar Monsalve: 18 (top); Colección Patricia Phelps de Cisneros: 25, 27, 29, 31, 36, 41, 72, 74, 101; Collection of Adriana Cisneros de Griffin: 76; © D21 Proyectos de Arte, Santiago de Chile: back cover (far left), 88; © Elena Damiani, image courtesy the artist and Revolver Galeria, Lima, photo Daniel Giannoni: 55; © Iran do Espírito Santo, image courtesy the artist, photo Eduardo Ortega: 94; © Thomaz Farkas Estate, images courtesy Thomaz Farkas / Instituto Moreira Salles Collection: 23; © Regina José Galindo: 22 (top), 49, photo Marlon García: 22 (top); © Sofía Gallisá Muriente, image courtesy the artist: back cover (center right), 90; © Mario García Torres: 58, 69, images courtesy the artist: 69; © Sheroanawë Hakihiiwë: 70, 71, 73; © Leandro Katz: 25, 27, 29, 31, image courtesy the artist: 25; © Gabriel Kuri: 53; © Maria Laet: 89; © David Lamelas: 91; © Suwon Lee: 41, 43, 45; © Anna Maria Maiolino, courtesy the artist and Hauser & Wirth, photo Regina Vater: 86; © Gilda Mantilla and Raimond Chaves: 33, image courtesy the artists, photo Eduardo Gonzalez: 20 (bottom); © Cildo Meireles: 65, 77, photo Thomas Griesel: 77; The Metropolitan Museum of Art, 18 (bottom); © Luis Molina-Pantin: front cover (far right), 39; © Aline Motta, images courtesy the artist: 80, 85; Montreal Museum of Fine Arts, photo Jean-François Brière: 38; Musée du quai Branly–Jacques Chirac, Dist. RMN–Grand Palais / Art Resource, NY, photo Vincent Mercier: 35; The Museum of Modern Art, New York, Department of Visual Resources: 9, 16, 37, 58, 68, 75, 89, 105, 107, photos Emile Askey: 39, 43, 45, 50, 65, 88, 95; Heidi Bohnenkamp: 103 (bottom); Robert Gerhardt: 61, 70, 71, 104 (top); Jonathan Muzikar: 53, 73, 104 (bottom); Mali Olatunji: 100 (bottom); Paul Salveson: 30; © Paulo Nazareth, images courtesy the artist and Mendes Wood DM: 82, 92; © Las Nietas de Nonó, images courtesy the artists: 66; © Roberto Obregón / Colección C&FE: 67; © Estate of Claudio Perna / Licensed by VAGA at Artists Rights Society (ARS), NY: front cover (center right), 37, 95; © Gala Porras-Kim, images courtesy the artist and Commonwealth and Council: 30; © Rosângela Rennó: front cover (far left), 93; © Mauro Restiffe, images courtesy the artist: 47; © José Alejandro Restrepo: 16, 18 (top), 35; © Thiago Rocha Pitta: front cover (center left), 9, 81, images courtesy the artist, photos Alyssa Miserendino: 81; © Analia Saban: 50, image courtesy the artist: 24 (top); © Daniel Steegmann Mangrané, photo Ricardo Bassetti: 76; © Michael Stevenson, image courtesy SculptureCenter, photo Julio Grinblatt: 51; Universidad Torcuato Di Tella, Departamento de Arte, photo Bruno Dubner: 33; © Adrián Villar Rojas, image courtesy the artist and Kurimanzutto: 36; Vrije Universiteit Amsterdam, Special Collections: 22 (bottom).

Just as the artists in *Chosen Memories: Contemporary Latin American Art from the Patricia Phelps de Cisneros Gift and Beyond* have engaged in dialogues across time and space, so have we looked far and wide in organizing this exhibition, which involved collaborating with many people inside and outside the Museum. My thanks go first to Patricia Phelps de Cisneros, for her unflagging support and truly inspiring generosity. This show honors her creative vision by bringing a core group of the works she has donated to MoMA into dialogue with other Latin American works from the collection.

I also extend my gratitude to the artists, who have not only enriched us with their work but have also shared their materials, ideas, and processes, as well as encouraging us to think further. Although this exhibition is drawn primarily from MoMA's collection, it also includes several selected loans. We thank the following lenders for entrusting the Museum with their works: Colección Patricia Phelps de Cisneros; Adriana Cisneros de Griffin; Anna Maria Maiolino and Hauser & Wirth; the Montreal Museum of Fine Arts; Alejandro Cesarco; Gala Porras-Kim and Commonwealth and Council; and Naufus Ramírez-Figueroa and Proyectos Ultravioleta. The exhibition also features a commissioned wall painting by Iran do Espírito Santo; I appreciate his enthusiasm for this project and the support of Fortes D'Aloia & Gabriel, his gallery in São Paulo.

At MoMA, Glenn D. Lowry, The David Rockefeller Director, has tirelessly championed the Patricia Phelps de Cisneros gift, and his trust and guidance have been key for the accomplishment of this exhibition and the accompanying publication. During an unprecedented few years of planning, we relied on the fearless leadership of Sarah Suzuki, Associate Director; Christy Thompson, Senior Deputy Director of Exhibitions and Collections; James Gara, Chief Operating Officer; Beverly Morgan-Welch, Senior Deputy Director of External Affairs; Nisa Mackie, The Edward John Noble Foundation Deputy Director of Learning and Audience Engagement; James Grooms, General Counsel and Secretary; Jay Levenson, Director of the International Program; and their brilliant teams. This undertaking was also supported by institutional programs, primarily the Patricia Phelps de Cisneros Research Institute for the Study of Art from Latin America, whose research on the Cisneros gift has been essential to the articulation of the project in writing as well as in the galleries. The extensive work done by former Cisneros Institute Research Fellow Madeline Murphy Turner, who interviewed almost all of the living artists included in the donation and contributed much to the early planning of the show, was crucial. The advice and counsel of María del Carmen Carrión, Project Manager of the Cisneros Institute, and the thorough research of Mellon-Marron Research Consortium Fellow Elise Chagas were also extremely valuable. Our research benefited from the rich resources of MoMA's Archives, Library, and Research Collections, and from the assistance of Jillian Suarez, Head of Library Services, and Ruth Halvey, the Patricia Phelps de Cisneros Bibliographer for Latin America, for which we are especially thankful.

The Latin American and Caribbean Fund has supported several important acquisitions included in the exhibition, and many more in the Museum's collection. I am profoundly grateful to Patricia Phelps de Cisneros, the fund's chair, and to each of its committed members. Thanks also go to Sylvia Renner, Associate Director, Affiliate Programs and International Funding, who lends special wit and expertise to the activities of the LACF. In the Department of Drawings and Prints, my home department, I appreciate the advocacy and collegiality of Robert Lehman Foundation Chief Curator Christophe Cherix, the expertise of my curatorial colleagues, and the invaluable support of the administrative team. I am also thankful for the collaboration of my colleagues in the Department of Painting and Sculpture, especially Marie-Josée and Henry Kravis Chief Curator Ann Temkin and Beverly Adams, Estrellita Brodsky Curator of Latin American Art; in the Department of Media and Performance, especially Lonti Ebers Chief Curator Stuart Comer for his eternal enthusiasm for Latin American art; and in the

Department of Photography (the best-represented department in this exhibition), especially former Joel and Anne Ehrenkranz Chief Curator Clément Chéroux. I am also grateful to Collection Specialists Emily Cushman (Drawings and Prints), Lily Goldberg (Painting and Sculpture), and Tasha Lutek (Photography), as well as to my colleagues Erica Papernik and Rebecca Kusovitsky in Media and Performance.

The dynamic process of planning this exhibition required the organization and cooperation of many capable minds and hands. Julia Detchon, Curatorial Assistant in the Department of Drawings and Prints, provided dedication, productive feedback, brilliant writing, and endless discretion throughout all phases of the project. It benefited, too, from the creative thinking of Exhibition Designer Hiroko Ishikawa and Exhibition Manager Elizabeth Henderson, the organization of Assistant Registrar Victoria Manning, and the thoughtful support of Lana Hum, Director of Exhibition Design and Production. Such a diverse selection of works required skillful treatment from conservators in every department, and I thank Anny Aviram, Lee Ann Daffner, Craig Kamrath, Lia Kramer, Laura Neufeld, Peter Oleksik, Magdalena Solano, and Lynda Zycherman for their consultation. Aaron Harrow and Mike Gibbons created an elegant and accessible audiovisual experience. Peter Perez expertly oversaw the framing of several key pieces, and Tom Krueger and Rob Jung safely transported and beautifully installed all of the works in the show. Claire Corey, Christie Zhong, and Kevin Ballon from the Creative Team designed a poetic visual identity for the exhibition. Olivia Oramas and Meg Montgoris, in Communications and Public Affairs, and Sarah Kennedy, Natalie Bedon, Sarah Bodinson, and Arlette Hernandez, in Learning and Engagement, helped to make the exhibition accessible to an international public.

In creating this catalogue, we are especially grateful for the rigorous guidance of the Publications Department, especially Don McMahon and Marc Sapir, but also Matthew Pimm, Hannah Kim, Curtis Scott, and Naomi Falk. The publication benefited from the careful eye of editor Kate Norment and the skillful translations of Kristina Cordero. Denis Doorly, Paul Abbey, and Jennifer Sellar, in addition to the talented photographers listed on the preceding pages, provided beautiful images for reproduction. The vision of Maricris Herrera of Estudio Herrera, Mexico City, and her colleague Israel Hernández brought the texts into lively dialogue with the works of art, and gave the entire project a distinctive identity.

Planning this exhibition involved a sustained collaboration with the Colección Patricia Phelps de Cisneros and its team. I want to thank Gabriel Pérez-Barreiro, Ileen Kohn, Alexa Halaby, Marcela Marcuso, and Camila Ocampo for their essential input and advice.

The brilliant selection of works by curators Sofía Hernández Chong Cuy, Paulo Herkenhoff, Luis Pérez-Oramas, and Gabriel Pérez-Barreiro, while working for the Colección Cisneros at different times in its history, is the foundation of this exhibition. All of these accomplished curators have, in their own way, changed the field of Latin American art in the process. To each of them, I express my great admiration. My hope is that *Chosen Memories*, a new reading of the Colección Cisneros in dialogue with its new institutional home, adds to the rich history of exhibitions they have organized over the years.

Finally, I am grateful to my friends and colleagues who brainstormed ideas and reviewed models and texts, especially Alejandro Cesarco, Eduardo Navarro, Nicolás Guagnini, Beto De Volder, Alejandra Seeber, Graciela Speranza, Santiago García Navarro, and León Villagrán. Thank you to all my New York friends who make life in this city warm and joyful.

Inés Katzenstein
Curator of Latin American Art and Director
of the Patricia Phelps de Cisneros Research
Institute for the Study of Art from Latin America

Major funding for the exhibition is provided by The International Council of The Museum of Modern Art.

Additional support is provided by the Annual Exhibition Fund. Leadership contributions to the Annual Exhibition Fund, in support of the Museum's collection and collection exhibitions, are generously provided by the Sandra and Tony Tamer Exhibition Fund, Sue and Edgar Wachenheim III, Jerry I. Speyer and Katherine G. Farley, Eva and Glenn Dubin, the Kate W. Cassidy Foundation, Anne Dias, Kenneth C. Griffin, Alice and Tom Tisch, the Marella and Giovanni Agnelli Fund for Exhibitions, Mimi Haas, The David Rockefeller Council, The Contemporary Arts Council of The Museum of Modern Art, Kathy and Richard S. Fuld, Jr., The International Council of The Museum of Modern Art, Marie-Josée and Henry R. Kravis, and Jo Carole and Ronald S. Lauder. Major contributions to the Annual Exhibition Fund are provided by Emily Rauh Pulitzer, The Sundheim Family Foundation, and Karen and Gary Winnick.

Published in conjunction with the exhibition *Chosen Memories: Contemporary Latin American Art from the Patricia Phelps de Cisneros Gift and Beyond*, organized by Inés Katzenstein, Curator of Latin American Art and Director of the Patricia Phelps de Cisneros Research Institute for the Study of Art from Latin America, and Julia Detchon, Curatorial Assistant in the Department of Drawings and Prints, at The Museum of Modern Art, New York, April 30–September 9, 2023.

Major funding for the exhibition is provided by The International Council of The Museum of Modern Art.

Additional support is provided by the Annual Exhibition Fund. Leadership contributions to the Annual Exhibition Fund, in support of the Museum's collection and collection exhibitions, are generously provided by the Sandra and Tony Tamer Exhibition Fund, Sue and Edgar Wachenheim III, Jerry I. Speyer and Katherine G. Farley, Eva and Glenn Dubin, the Kate W. Cassidy Foundation, Anne Dias, Kenneth C. Griffin, Alice and Tom Tisch, the Marella and Giovanni Agnelli Fund for Exhibitions, Mimi Haas, The David Rockefeller Council, The Contemporary Arts Council of The Museum of Modern Art, Kathy and Richard S. Fuld, Jr., The International Council of The Museum of Modern Art, Marie-Josée and Henry R. Kravis, and Jo Carole and Ronald S. Lauder. Major contributions to the Annual Exhibition Fund are provided by Emily Rauh Pulitzer, The Sundheim Family Foundation, and Karen and Gary Winnick.

Produced by the Department of Publications, The Museum of Modern Art, New York

Hannah Kim, Business and Marketing Director
Don McMahon, Editorial Director
Marc Sapir, Production Director
Curtis R. Scott, Associate Publisher

Edited by Kate Norment
Designed by Maricris Herrera and Israel Hernández, Estudio Herrera
Production by Matthew Pimm
Proofread by A. F. Dunlap Smith
Color separations by Verona Libri, Verona

Printed and bound by Verona Libri

This book is typeset in Unica77, Lector FSL, and Gopher. The paper is Condat Matte Perigord 150 gsm.

Published by The Museum of Modern Art
11 West 53 Street
New York, NY 10019-5497
www.moma.org

Inés Katzenstein's essay was translated from Spanish by Kristina Cordero.

Library of Congress Control Number: 2022948334

ISBN: 978-1-63345-138-4

Distributed in the United States and Canada by
ARTBOOK | D.A.P.
75 Broad Street
Suite 630
New York, NY 10004
www.artbook.com

Distributed outside the United States and Canada by
Thames & Hudson
181A High Holborn
London WC1V 7QX
www.thamesandhudson.com

Printed and bound in Italy

Front cover, left to right:
Rosângela Rennó. *Wedding Landscape*. 1996. (Page 93)
Thiago Rocha Pitta. *Herança* (*Heritage*). 2007. (Page 9)
Claudio Perna. *Haute Couture*. 1967–68. (Page 95)
Luis Molina-Pantin. *Mouse Pad*, from Nuevos paisajes (New Landscapes). 1999–2000. (Page 39)

Back cover, left to right:
Las Yeguas del Apocalipsis (Pedro Mardones Lemebel and Francisco Casas Silva). *Las dos Fridas* (*The Two Fridas*). 1989. (Page 88)
Laura Anderson Barbata. *Conejo*, from Intercambios, Amazonas Venezuela (Exchanges, Amazonas Venezuela). 1996–98. (Page 72)
Sofía Gallisá Muriente. *Asimilar y destruir* (*Assimilate and Destroy*). 2019. (Page 90)
Alejandro Cesarco. *Studies for a Series on Love* (*Wendy's Hands*). 2015. (Page 96)